KU-612-845

MA MURRAY

AMAZING STORIES

MA MURRAY

The Story of Canada's Crusty Queen of Publishing

HISTORY/BIOGRAPHY

by Stan Sauerwein

PUBLISHED BY ALTITUDE PUBLISHING CANADA LTD.
1500 Railway Avenue, Canmore, Alberta T1W 1P6
www.altitudepublishing.com
1-800-957-6888

Publisher   Stephen Hutchings
Associate Publisher   Kara Turner
Editor   Dianne Smyth

We acknowledge the financial support of the Government
of Canada through the Book Publishing Industry Development
Program (BPIDP) for our publishing activities.

Altitude GreenTree Program
Altitude Publishing will plant twice as many trees as were used
in the manufacturing of this product.

National Library of Canada Cataloguing in Publication Data

Sauerwein, Stan, 1952-
Ma Murray : the story of Canada's crusty queen of publishing / Stan
Sauerwein

(Amazing stories)
Includes bibliographical references.
ISBN 1-55153-979-9

1. Murray, Margaret L (Margaret Lally), 1888-1982. 2. Publishers and
publishing--Canada--Biography. 3. Journalists--Canada--Biography. I. Title.
II. Series: Amazing stories (Canmore, Alta.)
PN4913.M8S28 2003   070.92   C2003-910900-3

Printed and bound in Canada by Friesens
2 4 6 8 9 7 5 3 1

Cover: Ma Murray receiving the Order of Canada in 1971.

All photographs reproduced with kind permission from Margie Graham,
and Bain Gair of the *Bridge River—Lillooet News*

To Maggie and her coffee

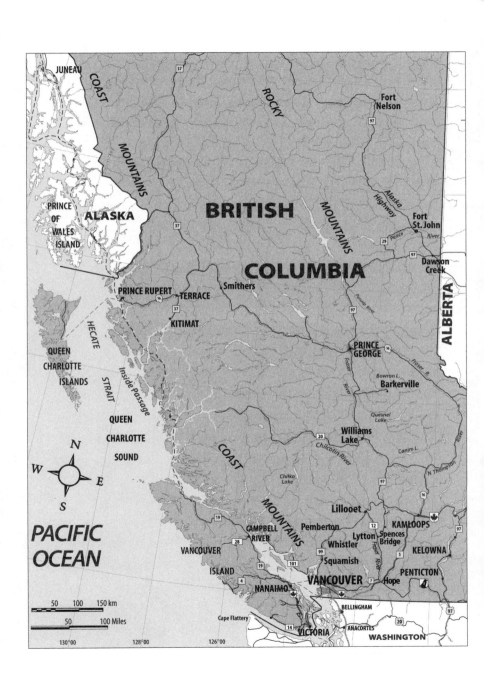

Contents

Prologue

The Cathay was a little too sporty for Margaret and George. Riding the elevator on the morning they moved, Margaret chatted with another guest. The two women were much alike. Neither had a problem finding words to describe the horrific squalor just a few feet from the hotel door.

The American navy would soon be spiriting away her lift companion, Eleanor Roosevelt, from the clawing sea of refugees swarming into Shanghai. Margaret was facing a longer sentence. Her husband, a British Columbia MLA, was on a trade mission. They had planned a visit talking with government and industry leaders that could last months.

When she met the U.S. president's wife, Margaret was in the process of moving the Murray belongings to the Metropole three blocks away. The room cost half as much but the view from the terrace was twice as unsettling. Alleys around her new hotel were glutted with refugees. The streets were so clogged with the frightened and displaced that a beater had to cut a swath through the crowds with a cane.

"I can't say which is weakening most, my hands or my thumping heart," she wrote afterwards. To their dismay, Shanghai had become a war zone the day they decided to move. On August 14, 1937, two Chinese planes swooped below the heavy cloud cover over Shanghai. Intending to bomb the battleship Idzuma, *the pilots accidentally dropped their charges on the streets of Shanghai — only a few hundred yards from the Cathay.*

Margaret, who witnessed the devastation from her balcony, wretched on the stench of cordite and feverishly tried to record what she saw for her newspaper back home. "We'll sleep in the closet till morning. If there is a morning," she wrote. "The water and power are off. Every word impressed on these keys is a prayer, but now I can't see. George has the flashlight out and the Bible turned to the fourteenth Chapter of John...."

Chapter 1
A Pen and a Promise

She was born on a tidy farm outside Windy Ridge, Kansas on a hot August 3rd in 1888, the seventh wailing voice to join the Lally household choir.

Margaret (Peg) had a raw Irish vitality that surfaced as strong will, fearlessness, and generosity. Taken in pieces each of these traits made her wonderfully engaging. Together they gave her an explosive personality that earned her a prophetic nickname from the time she could crawl. "Trouble-the-house" taxed her parents' patience and meddled in her siblings' games. As a child her inquisitive face eagerly appeared wherever she wasn't wanted and went missing wherever she was.

She was attractive, though just short of pretty, and buxom by the age of 12. She had brown curly hair and an even set of white teeth that filled her wide mouth when she smiled. Built from the firebrand genes of her Rebel County ancestors in Cork, she refused to flee barnyard tussles like her sisters did. She learned to defend herself and regularly dissuaded the unwanted attentions of randy farmhands, who often surprised her in the tall corn, with a stiff right cross or an upraised knee.

Margaret Lally had a pioneer's heart. She was as handy castrating pigs as the most experienced man on the farm and could endure cyclones with unbroken faith, so long as a rosary was at hand. While she knew how to scratch life from the parched Kansas earth, her experience with books and what they contained was decidedly lacking.

Peg showed a distinct dislike for injustice at an early age. She quit school at age 13 over a spilled corn incident. On the day she quit, pupils in the one-room school had been tossing kernels of corn and Margaret Lally got the blame. The teacher demanded she clean up the mess after school. Margaret did, putting each kernel in her flour sack apron until she'd gathered every one. When she was done she opened the door and faced the teacher. "Here you are, Ma'am!" she yelled and with the shout — snapped the apron open — showering the classroom and the startled teacher.

Peg "ran like hell" and never returned to master the mysteries of punctuation or vowels and consonants. Her lack of education was a definite constraint in finding work, even at the end of the nineteenth century. For more than four years, Margaret struggled to support herself independently, most often settling for low paying positions as an unappreciated house-girl in kitchens across western Kansas. She learned to face the lowly treatment she often received with silence instead of a cuss and she adopted a philosophical attitude towards hardship.

At 17, when her sister Bess had already graduated from teacher's college, Peg decided she'd had enough of nasty farmwives and soiled dungarees. She sewed herself a wardrobe and enrolled in a business school in Freemont, Nebraska. It was the first evidence of the stubborn streak she would show in the future when the odds piled high and seemed to put success beyond the reach of anyone (but her).

Practically penniless, she convinced the school to accept "sweat equity" and worked off her tuition with hours in the kitchen. Within a year she managed to get a grasp on the fine art of typing, filing, shorthand, and bookkeeping. She was ready to seek her fortune in an

From left to right, Bess, Margaret, and Delia Lally

office instead of a farmhouse. Grammar still eluded her, but typing and figures came with little effort and in short order she found a job as a bookkeeper for the Shipley Saddlery and Mercantile Company in Kansas City.

Margaret harboured a romantic nature and with each saddle that left the store she dreamed of the tanned Alberta cowpunchers who would soon be riding in them. She imagined them, strong and stoic, young and handsome, and devised a way of reaching out to her imaginary prairie knights by tucking notes in with the invoices. Over the summer the six girls in the firm's shipping department found themselves the happy recipients of cards, letters, and photographs from strapping prospects with walrus mustaches and weathered features.

By spring Margaret had decided she simply must find a way to Alberta where she could lure one of the prize prospects in person. Her sister, tall, slim schoolteacher Bess, had shared the winter evenings reviewing the pictures and letters with equal interest. She decided Margaret had the right idea and went along. Their plan was to work their way from Kansas to the Pacific Ocean and then along the west coast to Canada. They left on their quest giddy and excited, boarding a west-bound train with little more than a vague notion of what might be waiting ahead.

Ma Murray

In rainy Seattle they immediately found part-time work as typists and just as quickly learned that Kansas flowers droop in the liquid sunshine. Both girls suffered bouts of pneumonia and rheumatism. Their first grim winter was spent sharing a damp bed-sitting room that reeked of respiratory ointment. During one of Margaret's more healthy periods she decided moving time had arrived. She bought a ticket on a Canadian steamship to Vancouver and with a flurry of energy, $15 in cash, and promises to send for Bess as soon as she could, she headed north.

Within three days, Bess had a letter from her sister. Everything was "peachy," Margaret confided. She had talked a hotelkeeper into providing a room in exchange for making beds and promised to begin the hunt "for more-fitten jobs" right away.

Vancouver was foreign turf, a puzzlement to the young woman and she reported each case of strangeness to her sister. In the first place traffic ran on the wrong side of the street. Newspapers looked funny. All the policemen she'd seen wore droopy mustaches. "It's real ding-dong up here," she concluded, "but somehow I like it and I think you will. You can't help it. It's sorta romantic. People talk softer and they treat you nice. I can't get over the birds singing, fit to burst their throats. It makes you want to know what's behind those lovely mountains, and what's on the other side of that ocean. Oh, and the trees! They're just like the men — big — they reach almost to heaven. Be a good girl and remember, even if I am in redcoat territory, I'm less than two hundred miles from you. So don't be lonesome...."

Vancouver was one of the fastest growing cities in Canada in 1912. It had attracted the dreamers and the doers, European aristocrats and American promoters, miners and lumberjacks, fishermen and storekeepers. Incorporated by 1000 positive-thinking pioneers only 24 years earlier, it had ballooned to 100,000 souls by the time young Margaret stepped onto the docks. In every direction the sound of hammers marked daylight as surely as any rooster. There was a real estate agent for every 150 people. A third of the residents were immigrants and it showed in the variety of restaurants and saloons, and in the various languages she heard on the street corners.

Synchronistically shaping the rest of her life, Margaret's first job was selling subscriptions to a new trade paper that was hitting the streets for the first time just as she arrived from Seattle. The *B.C. Federationist* represented labour but Margaret didn't let that stop her from picking the very den of big business (on the two top floors of the largest office building in Vancouver) as her sales territory. To doctors she argued that patients would welcome the read while they waited on appointments. To lawyers she pitched the paper's news about what was worrying business. And to businessmen she promised insider knowledge about what the workers were cooking up. In a day she'd covered the waiting rooms with the *B.C. Federationist* sheets (at $1.50 for two years) and was happily counting her commissions.

But selling subscriptions wouldn't do for Bess, so Margaret kept up the job hunt. She registered with the Underwood Agency, a placement firm that found work for freelance secretaries, and was given the odd typing assignment downtown before she was offered a job no one else wanted to take.

South Vancouver, the agency's placement secretary said, was the fastest growing neighbourhood in town. Maybe 16 kilometres by streetcar... it was "rural"... but a newspaperman from the east had decided it needed a paper. The job to keep the books for him paid only $12 a week, she reported, but it was a permanent position. Was Margaret interested? She literally leapt at the offer.

George Matheson Murray, the man she was to meet in South Vancouver, was an oatmeal porridge Scot as Canadian as maple syrup. Brown-eyed and of gentle disposition, he was a stocky and handsome barrel-chested fellow who'd grown up in Woodstock, Ontario. He had cut his journalistic teeth at the *Ottawa Journal*.

A Pen and a Promise

George was bright and well educated and he'd formed (since childhood) deep loyalties for the Liberal Party's political vision of Canada. While working his way to the west, reporting for newspapers in Regina and Edmonton, he'd come to the realization that Canada needed men of political vision. Men who were capable of imagining the incredible future of the Dominion. He wanted to be part of that political will and saw newspapers as a stepping-stone to government life. In his estimation, the west coast was the kind of place where a young man with energy could shoulder his way into the corridors of political power. George had made his way to Vancouver along with the thousands of other eager settlers who crammed the transcontinental railway passenger cars from eastern Canada.

As soon as he arrived, young Murray ranged over the city looking for a place to settle. His uncle, Ken Murray, had reached Vancouver years before and become a heavy investor in the development of the southern slope. George was certain this development would continue but when he approached his uncle for help in establishing himself, the older man scoffed at his nephew's intentions.

"May God bless me," he said mirthlessly. "You want to get into politics?" Ken Murray had trouble dealing with anyone who didn't see business as the basis for success and happiness. It was especially vexing because the young newspaperman seemed to be shunning what Ken Murray believed was every Scot's natural bent. He didn't want money! All George sought was his uncle's willingness to recommend him to his colleagues once he managed to start a newspaper. Reluctantly his uncle agreed and in May 1912, George opened the doors to the city's newest paper. The *South Vancouver Chinook* had a long list of potential advertisers.

After an hour of stops and starts, Margaret stepped off the trolley at the end of the Main Street carline and surveyed her surroundings. South Vancouver definitely was as close to country as she'd seen since Windy Ridge. On either side of the dirt street, wooden boardwalks stretched for blocks. The raw wet stumps of trees marked the road like sentries, broken in their sequence by unruly patches of bracken and the freshly built wooden boxes that made up the homes and businesses of South Vancouver. There was a dairy, a school, a butcher shop, and a municipal hall. The community seemed to have the same buzz of activity she'd seen in the downtown streets of Vancouver.

The offices of Greater Vancouver Publishers were a five-block walk from the end of the line. Margaret adjusted herself before entering the offices and tried to put on as staid an appearance as she could. After all, she'd heard newspapers were serious places and she wanted to begin with the right impression.

On entering however, her hopes were immediately deflated. The office was small, almost as small as the tiny paper she scanned at the counter. George Murray however, lightly tapping at the keys of his typewriter, did hold some promise, she thought. Margaret took in his image with an appraising eye. He had an almost cultured appearance with gold cufflinks and watch chain glinting in the sunlight.

George introduced himself and then formally questioned Margaret about her experience. Not to be sidetracked, because her experience was limited to selling subscriptions for the *B.C. Federationist,* Margaret replied with questions of her own.

"Tell me about this newspaper of yours. Does it have many accounts?"

"Check for yourself," George happily replied. Her interest in his dream was all it took for the young publisher to launch into a description of the potential he saw for the paper. He shook open a copy that had been on his desk and held it up for her to read. "By George, great, eh?"

Margaret tried to hide her own lack of enthusiasm. This was just another of those funny newspapers she'd

A young George Murray

already told Bess about. It had more grey type than advertising and was a flimsy 12-page example at that. She couldn't understand what the fuss was about when the publisher enthusiastically described it as if it were the *Kansas City Post*. Still, she wanted the job and thought spending more time with this "good looker" might pay an additional dividend or two.

George explained how the *Chinook* needed a book-keeper immediately. His company was backed by an active group of Vancouver real estate promoters eager to attract more residents. They planned on extensive advertising and would keep his press (recently rescued from printing salmon can wrappers) quite busy as the paper grew.

Margaret dickered. A $12 per week pay cheque would not be enough. Tram ride tickets would quickly add up, she added, with an accountant's sensibility. If he was willing to increase the pay to $18 a week she could consider the daily jaunt. "Let's roll some dice and see who wins," she suggested.

George was taken aback. He boosted the pay offer to $15 a week and Margaret agreed, in return, to add collections and subscription sales to her duties. "Done," George happily confirmed, extending a large, well-groomed hand to hers. "You start Monday." He passed her the copy of his second edition and went back to the typewriter.

Margaret took to her job with enthusiasm, but life in South Vancouver wasn't going to be an easy slide to prosperity for the Lally sisters. Unbeknownst to her or anyone else, the tremendous boom gripping the west coast had petered out. Within a short time the street outside the *Chinook* would become lonely and quiet. Economic recession seemed to take people by surprise because it crept over the country within months of the 1911 election. American capital fled Canada following the Borden Conservative Party's leap to power, leaving Vancouver with soup kitchens and unemployment in its wake.

South Vancouver's growth — which had seen an incomparable expansion with entire neighbourhood developments selling out in a day — stopped dead in its tracks. The enthusiastic setting quickly turned into a hotbed of political debate as residents who'd invested in the area (expecting municipal services to follow) got a rude awakening. They wanted the streetcar lines extended and sewer and water lines installed, but the government didn't have the finances. The public angrily accused officials of graft and the weekly *Chinook* was a visible cheerleader in the centre of the debate. It offered them strong editorial opinion and sensational reports of municipal meetings that roused their ire more with every issue.

Margaret took to the controversy, avidly reading George's galleys and gaining a growing sense of awe for his writing ability and his views. She arrived early for work and often left late, with barely enough time to catch the last tram for Vancouver. She accepted any task willingly, from bookkeeping to advertising sales, and learned that a little ingenuity went a long way when it came to selling white space.

To flog ads for the Highland Games she learned enough about the Scots to pass for one herself. Peg learned enough about beef grades and shipment woes to converse with the butcher. She could describe Dr. Sun Yat-sen's failed coup in China with Lum Fat at the laundry as if she herself lived in Vancouver's Shanghai Alley. Everything about the newspaper business was fresh to her and she eagerly soaked up the experiences while she saved enough money to bring Bess to Vancouver. Despite the excitement that Margaret found in this fascinating world of ink and type however, Bess never let her lose sight of their original mission. "The good lookers with John B. Stetson hats are still riding the horizon out there around Calgary," she reminded Margaret, once the two were together again. With a few more months of saving, Bess calculated they'd have enough to head east, but her sister had become less enthusiastic.

The news bug had bitten Margaret. George Murray allowed her the privilege of writing up some of the church happenings and community announcements for the paper. It was all gossip that she easily gathered on trips into Collingwood when she was collecting ads. As his own reporting load grew George extended her warrant to reporting on political meetings and ratepayers' rallies.

She described her new duties in letters to family in Kansas. "For a little newspaper, it's sure exciting. My boss is a nice young man, a little vague and annoying maybe, but real handsome. He loves this country so much and talks so much about northern British Columbia that you forget what time it is and listen. The other afternoon we walked clear to Broadway — twenty-four long blocks — before I remembered to catch a streetcar."

It was obvious that Margaret was fairly smitten by the young publisher, but George seemed uninterested. She had no idea how wrong that impression was, but it was his lack of attention that finally pushed Margaret back towards thoughts of Bess and Alberta.

While the *Chinook*'s outspoken political viewpoints helped it grow in popularity in South Vancouver, advertising was still a major chore in the depressed economy. To boost their fortunes, George occasionally called upon freelance sales groups to help him produce special reports and Margaret was pressed into service to assist them. Her wide appeal as a friend to many an advertiser was quickly recognized by one of the groups and they offered her a chance to work with them on an Alberta assignment.

The day before Christmas 1912, Margaret told George she would be moving on.

George was stricken but didn't show his disappointment. In the few days remaining before an early January departure, Margaret helped collect payments for advertising, arguing pointlessly when the publisher let failing businesses squeeze out from under the burden of their debt to his paper. In Margaret's eyes, George's kindness was a frustrating and even annoying trait that whispered of his own bankruptcy if he didn't change his ways.

On her last day, as she cleared the final letters and invoices from her desk, George asked her into his office. He asked her one last time if she would reconsider and Margaret answered with certainty that she'd made her decision. Sadly he held out his fountain pen and asked her to take it. "I want you to remember me, and write. Will you promise to do that?"

Margaret was unsure about accepting such an expensive gift, but George's soft manner convinced her it was okay. With tears welling, she promised to correspond and then left quickly before the words her heart demanded could be spoken.

Chapter 2
Of Publishing and Politics

The residents of Calgary do a schizo-phrenic dance with their wardrobes during winter. Just as soon as they grow accustomed to icy Arctic temperatures, nature does a flip. In a few hours winter can turn to spring while the city is clutched in the warm, moisture-starved embrace of the Chinook winds. The winds dive over the Rockies, heralded by a sweeping arch of blue sky that appears with cookie-cutter sharpness in the gray winter horizon. Heavy coats are shed. The snow vanishes. The streets turn to mud.

But in January 1913 when Margaret arrived with

Of Publishing and Politics

Charlie Fuller and his wife Katey to sell advertising for the *Albertan,* Calgary wasn't being warmed by those winds. It was frigid and inhospitable and the trio's wardrobe was decidedly unsuitable. They stood out from the crowd of hardy Calgarians who were dressed in heavy coats, scarves, and mitts, like blossoms among snowdrifts.

To make matters worse, the *Albertan* had changed its mind. Charlie Fuller immediately took to the streets to find them another assignment. Within a day he'd located another newspaper, the *Labour Statesman,* that was interested in their services. Katey and Margaret were happy to relax in warmth at the King Edward Hotel and wait for their next assignment. Their temporary home, just a block from the ruins of old Fort Calgary, was less expensive than the posh Canadian Pacific Railway hotel that loomed beside the train depot two kilometres to the west.

On the afternoon of their second day in the city, Charlie met with the *Statesman*'s publisher and the women planned on shopping for clothes that matched the weather. Unfortunately, while Charlie was pitching the rosy financial potential of newspaper supplements, he suffered a heart attack. Instead of visiting dry goods stores, the two women found themselves tensely waiting at Holy Cross Hospital for word about Charlie.

By the next day, Charlie was stable and visitors were allowed. He told Katey and Margaret that the doctor had given him dire warnings about working and had prescribed three months of bed rest. The Fullers needed Margaret's help. To cover the hospital bill and to pay for the train ride back to their home in Seattle, they needed money. Charlie asked Margaret to return to Vancouver and collect on some delinquent accounts. Their future depended on her wily ability to extract money from slow-paying customers. Margaret agreed immediately and was on the next west-bound train.

When she arrived back in more temperate climes, George was waiting on the platform. He'd been notified of her arrival by telegram. He was ecstatic. "The *Chinook* is a morgue without you," he said, vigorously shaking her hand. Now that she was in Vancouver again, he told her, he didn't intend to let her leave.

"I'm going right back," Margaret emphatically stated. "I just came out to collect some money so that Katey can take Charlie back to Seattle." George was disappointed. "Have dinner with me tonight, Margaret, and let's talk this over." Margaret reluctantly agreed, telling him no matter what he had to say, she intended to do just as she'd been asked and return to Calgary within a week bearing the $500 debt she'd come to collect.

When she was reunited with Bess that day at the

Dunsmuir Hotel, the women discussed what had happened and the meaning of George Murray's insistent invitation. Bess said she could see just how much Margaret was in love with the young publisher by the way she described their meeting at the train station. Bess was certain the two were meant to be together.

Margaret disagreed, adamantly telling her sister nothing romantic existed between them. "God's truth, how could there be? I've hardly said six words to the guy in all these months. He does the talking, and it's mostly about railroads, politics, and how he'd like to go to the Peace River corridor, wherever the hell that is. Besides, he's a Presbyterian, and his folks are pretty uppity. They'll have a rich girl all picked out for him."

Bess let Margaret borrow her finest hat for the dinner date with George at the Hotel Vancouver. After they were seated, George again confessed how he missed the Kansas girl in his life and that he desperately wanted her to stay in Vancouver.

"Mr. Murray, I explained about Mr. Fuller. I can't go back on my word, and him so sick and all."

"Nobody wants you to go back on your word," George replied with a cagey smile. He ordered their meal, steaks *a la briande*, and they talked about Calgary and Charlie's health while they waited for their supper. "You can't know how I've missed you. You had to go away for me to realize how cheerful and light-hearted you are, and what an effect you had around the office."

Margaret tried to brush off the flattery.

"Margaret, I'm really trying to tell you something else. I'm trying to tell you that I want you to marry me."

She was stunned and recited a litany of reasons why such a match was doomed to failure. She was just a clerk and he was a publisher. She was a Catholic and he a Presbyterian. Their families would have a fit.

"Well, your mother isn't marrying me, and you're not marrying my aunts, so why bring that up?"

"I only went to Grade 3 in school. Look at you! You got nice manners, and good taste — you want to be a senator for goodness sakes!"

George only smiled. He could see Margaret was only looking for a way to say yes. He told her he didn't expect her to change her religion any more than she would expect that of him. He said he didn't love her because she was educated or rich, but precisely because she was the opposite.

"Marry me."

Margaret felt herself melt in the gaze from his kind brown eyes.

The next day was Ash Wednesday, February 5, 1913, a day of mourning for devout Catholics. It found George up early and on the telephone with Archbishop Timothy

Casey, arranging for an appointment that afternoon. He also called his printer Bert Stein at the *Chinook* and asked him to get his wife Gertrude from their home in Collingwood and to meet him at the archbishop's residence. He didn't say why, just that they had to be on time.

When Bert and his wife arrived at the residence after a six hour horse-drawn cab ride from Collingwood, they learned of the reason from Margaret and were incredulous.

"Married to George? Look, kiddo, don't talk like that. That bird isn't getting married. I mean, he just isn't the…well…the marrying kind." Margaret just shrugged. "Well, whatever kind he is, I'm marrying him, I guess."

George confirmed it, waving an envelope that contained the archbishop's hard won permission for their union. "We have an hour-and-a-half to get downtown to the cathedral," George said, herding them all into the street. He'd timed the ceremony and celebration with military precision, the Holy Rosary Cathedral and a special dinner afterwards at the Elyseum Hotel. Raising glasses of expensive champagne provided by Bob Edwards, publisher of the *Calgary Eye-Opener* after the wedding, George toasted their future and predicted a long, happy, and no doubt interesting life together. The cathedral bells, chiming in the distance, seemed to signal that heaven concurred.

Ma Murray

Though the obligatory introduction of the bride to George's relatives was met with cool politeness and an unsaid disapproval, the couple agreed to rent an apartment from George's uncle where they could begin their life together. Ken Murray had felt the impact of the economic collapse in Vancouver. An apartment building he had been constructing was not yet finished because of a lack of funds, but would suffice for the newlyweds. In spite of the uncomfortable prospect of having almost daily interaction with Uncle Ken and his hammer, and weekly visits by George's prim aunts, Margaret dutifully agreed to the arrangement because it helped the family purse. Then she immediately got pregnant.

Margaret spent the next nine months in discomfort, suffering both nausea and the unwelcome attention of George's aunts. When the baby arrived, the boy they'd hoped for turned out to be the opposite sex. But Georgina (Georgie) was a blessing nonetheless. And the Murrays needed any blessed help they could get. By the time the war broke out in August 1914, South Vancouver's economic situation was a disaster. Even to the richest man, a dollar had become very dear. In taverns talk about the Canadian Banking Act was more common than talk about the weather.

George and his friend, a young lawyer named Gerald McGeer, often met at the Murray apartment bemoaning the state of the province's affairs. George was adamant that change was required. What the province needed was some direction. It needed lower freight rates. It needed to keep step, and with a provincial election looming, it needed a man like George. McGeer pledged to speak on his friend's behalf if George would agree to stand for the Liberal nomination in South Vancouver.

As a new wife and mother, Margaret was dismayed by the prospect of election expenses. The amount of time that a good campaign effort demanded was also a concern for her because she was already pregnant again. And, though she didn't really fathom the Canadian political system she was certain that winning an election was expensive. There was the cost of the promotional printing for one thing, she said. What about that? George confidently told her not to worry. "I have backers," he said. He told her the *Chinook* would do the printing and bill the supporters after his inevitable nomination was secured.

Margaret reluctantly agreed to support him. She understood how deep the desire to be involved in politics ran in George. She had fallen in love with her young husband's dreams too and promised she'd help with his campaigning as long as she didn't have to do so in the morning.

Campaign they did. Relentlessly. For weeks. Margaret dragged out the pram, and with Georgina in it, pushed it in a pregnant waddle on visits to every card-carrying Liberal she could find in South Vancouver. When it came time for the vote, a large group of party members gathered for the South Vancouver nomination meeting. They were eager and ready to fight the Conservative government. They were fed up with the war and the soup kitchens, and tired of rising taxes without the balancing compensation of payrolls. Margaret had heard it all and knew her husband had solutions in mind for everything.

True to his word, McGeer stood and spoke for the publisher candidate. His nomination speech began slowly. He believed in George and started to list the waiting nominee's credentials. But McGeer was too emotionally invested himself in the need for political change. With a rising level of enthusiasm, he explored the ideas the two men had discussed over so many nights in George's kitchen. He attacked the unfair banking act, the freight rates, and the deplorable lack of vision he saw coming from the ruling McBride government. He was a rolling thunderhead of rousing oratory and when it came time to actually name George for the nomination, the crowd was in a shambles. They stamped their feet in accord with every statement

McGeer shouted. They clapped enthusiastically and called out in agreement like a Holy Rollers church congregation.

Not surprisingly, someone stood in the audience, and loudly nominated McGeer from the floor. Within seconds someone else moved for a vote and in a unanimous sea of upraised hands, McGeer was bestowed with their trust and the nomination.

It was a devastating turn of events but Margaret put on a brave face for George. Then she used the private nest egg she had been saving for a new pair of shoes in order to pay for the hall rental.

In the months that followed, the Murray financial picture looked bleak. George's uncle, who also felt the economic pinch, was pressuring for rent. Along with the expense for the election posters and handouts printed prior to the nomination, the couple needed to keep their only trickle of income flowing. The payroll at the *Chinook* often consumed the entire advertising profit. Putting food on the table became a test of endurance. How long could they eat rice with milk, raisins, and brown sugar, or soup, or porridge at every meal before the family's health suffered? Margaret did her best, baking brown bread and making jams from fruit she hand-picked and canned. Luxuries such as butter and meat were not included in her larder.

George tried to augment the family income by free-lancing for the daily newspapers in Vancouver, and after a particularly poor period of sales at the *Chinook*, he joined forces with an old friend on a speculative news-paper venture. Joseph Martin, then a King's Counsel, also had a dream relating to British Columbia politics. He'd already served as an MP (Member of Parliament) in both England and Canada. As premier of British Columbia for less than four months during 1900, he'd helped establish the eight-hour workday across the country. In 1916 he saw a chance for a Liberal resurgence, but to form a new government he needed the support of the press and ample publicity for his political platform. His solution was to set up a newspaper of his own.

With George contributing some of the machinery and working as the editor, Joe Martin opened the *Vancouver Evening Journal* in a city already served by two other dailies. As a politician, Martin was one of British Columbia's bright lights but as a publisher he was a failure. He immediately learned how difficult it was to sell white space in the depressed Vancouver economy and had to turn to his brother, a partner in a wholesale drug firm in Winnipeg, for ads.

George was trying to launch a competitive news alternative, but Martin could only sell pitches for items such as syphilis cures and impotency aids. Martin tried selling shares in his venture, and succeeded in attracting some investors, but not enough of them. Within weeks the sheriff had padlocked the doors and George was again demoralized, feeling his bad luck was somehow evidence of a weak character. He hadn't enlisted in the war, choosing to stay and make good on his debts, and this too haunted the patriotic newsman.

Margaret's maternal instincts were roused. The brilliant man she'd married hadn't been hardened as she had been. He hadn't been raised to expect the cycles of disappointment or despair that were so often the lot of a poor Kansas farmer. Once again, she put a courageous face on the circumstances. She counselled her husband not to give in to his depression. It was the same offer of hope her mother had provided her father every time cyclones or hail or drought spoiled another crop.

"You still have the *Chinook...*" she reminded him. "Something will turn up." With a hug and a kiss she planted some Irish luck in his shirt pocket and encouraged him to carry on. As if the "pixie dust" was real, things changed in two ways.

The same pale economy that was grinding them down provided a brief respite for the Murrays and the *Chinook.* It came in the form of tax-sale lists that needed to be published by the municipal clerk in South

Vancouver. George produced the only newspaper of record for South Vancouver and so for a short period the *Chinook* was stable again with a $7000 injection in Legal Ads.

It meant the couple could settle some old debts. Margaret found a nursemaid for Dan, their second baby, shipped Georgie to George's aunts for a while, and took on the bookkeeping at the paper. Now that she was back, she vowed never again to leave the business to be a homemaker. Margaret had married to be George's life partner and to her that meant newspapers.

George's run of bad luck had shaken his confidence in the future, so Margaret used every chance she had to boost his self-esteem. When George learned of parcels of crown land to be had above the shores of Burrard Inlet east of Vancouver (by anyone willing to clear the land and homestead) she encouraged him to borrow the $10 deposit from Joe Martin and file. But deep inside, she suspected the opportunity was too good to be true.

Their first visit was a weekend camping trip. Early one Saturday morning, the entire family boarded the Howe Sound Navigation Company's ship, the *New Delta* along with a band of other "settlers" going on a two-hour ride from the Dunlevy Street dock. The purpose of the excursion was to inspect the eight hectares George had registered. When they finally arrived, at what is now the Imperial Oil refinery at Ioco, Margaret's doubts were confirmed.

Getting to the property required a long walk on the floating dock to the beach and then a two-and-a-half kilometre hike uphill. "In the name of God, how long is this hill?" Margaret asked angrily as she lugged a suitcase of camping gear up the incline and tried to keep her husband in sight. Baby Dan, nestled in a packsack on her back like an Irish papoose, was wailing to be fed. Georgina, perched on her father's shoulders, was counting trees.

"The land lies in the valley above, my dear," George replied. "Listen to the birds! Smell that good air!" Where exactly the birds were singing was a mystery to Margaret as she scrambled to follow. She had to keep her head down to pick her path through the brush, swat clouds of voracious mosquitoes, and try to soothe the babe with her voice all at the same time. When they reached the property they intended to claim, George was beaming with pride but Margaret shrugged in disbelief.

They'd arrived at a moonscape of clear-cut forest. The area was littered with blackened stumps, salmonberry bushes, and thistles. Without the trees to shelter their tiny patch of valley, Vancouver's rains had washed away most of the topsoil, leaving acres of what looked like river bottom. "Well," Margaret said, "the price is right."

She listened to George's descriptions of what they could make of their home site. During the many weekends that followed she never complained. Together they raised a cottage, began land clearing, stump pulling, and garden planting. Margaret accepted the chores willingly. It was precisely the life Margaret had left in Kansas but she loved being able to work alongside her husband and talk about something other than politics. That summer the homestead became more than a lark for the couple whom their neighbours openly described as crazy city folk.

And while they managed to invest $1000 in the property out of newspaper income, the pressure it caused on the family purse was staggering. By the summer of 1919, George was forced to sell the *Chinook* so more of the newspaper's start-up debt could be fully repaid. The tarpaper-covered cabin, nestled on the half hectare they'd cleared, was all George had to show for his efforts with the *Chinook*. Without that job to keep him busy however, Margaret saw a chance to get away from it all. She talked George into making a trip to visit her aging parents in Kansas.

George wasn't enthusiastic but he bent to Margaret's request. Once in the United States he landed a job as a reporter at the *Kansas City Post* and the family moved into a boarding house, their new home in the

American city. Margaret's sister Bess, who had come to Canada with her, was by now back in the United States and working for executives at General Motors in Detroit. Margaret eagerly renewed acquaintances with the rest of her "people." But, her happiness was cut short soon after they arrived.

Influenza was raging across the countryside and Margaret fell gravely ill with the disease. Because the hospitals were already filled to capacity, she was treated at the boarding house throughout the slow process of recovery. She survived but she was severely weakened. She had trouble walking and couldn't bathe herself. Reluctantly she told George the visit had been a mistake. "Take me home darling," she said. "I want to go home."

George was incredulous. He'd walked away from everything in Canada on Margaret's whim and now she was flipping everything on its side again. Without a job in Canada or a suitable place to live, it seemed ludicrous. But he deeply loved Margaret and agreed, perhaps fearing it might be his wife's last request. Months after they'd loaded themselves onto the *New Delta* for their American holiday, they returned to the homestead. Margaret's sister Anne agreed to come along to care for her. Margaret, bedraggled and frail, was so weak she had to be transported up the hill in a wagon.

Jobless and desperately poor, the couple found

creative ways to manage. George secured a partial car-load of flour from a friend and bartered it for vegetables from the gardens of other settlers in the neighbourhood just so they could eat. While Margaret recovered at the homestead with the help of Anne, George stayed with his uncle in Vancouver during the week and worked for wages at the *Vancouver Province*. The family's penury lasted for two years.

In 1921 however, George finally had a change in fortune. He hurried to the homestead mid-week. And because the *New Delta* wasn't making a run that day, he rowed across Burrard Inlet to tell Margaret the good news. He was taking over the managing editor's job at the *Vancouver Morning Sun* for Robert J. Cromie, he told her. Things were finally looking up.

Years earlier, Margaret had met Cromie when she delivered printing that the *Chinook* had churned out for the company where Cromie worked (as an accountant). Cromie, a sandy-haired dynamo, became a legend in newspaper circles in Vancouver. He was half financial wizard and half rogue and he handled his editors with the compassion of an unenlightened Ebenezer Scrooge.

While the position at the paper was more fitting with George's experience as a newspaperman, it didn't bring with it an enviable salary. Still, it was more than they'd had in the family kitty for some time. There was enough for them to move back to Vancouver and rent a house at Templeton and Hastings. The home was a dreary little frame cottage in which former tenants had kept chickens in the kitchen, but it was better than the leaky homestead.

Cromie had cleverly managed to buy the city's only Liberal-supporting newspaper when its finances were at low ebb. He worked relentlessly to build it with advertising promotions that sometimes leaned to the ridiculous. He put a heavy arm on Liberal Party backers and was not afraid to appeal for ad payments well in advance of publication. He set the newspaper on a secure footing, but that required a blind eye to the low-value pay slips he gave his reporters and editors. He didn't demand a high standard for writing, especially if it was going to cost him more money — and he was just as apt to fire a reporter as he was to praise him.

George Murray grudgingly put up with the affront to his own standards because it meant a job. Gradually and laboriously he built a trained and polished news crew on a slim editorial budget. But his time at the newspaper was filled with moments of deep unease. Finally, when Cromie decided to promote a so-called "healer" called Crepo — even after the Vancouver medical establishment had called the man a fake — George could take it no more. He quit.

Fed up with not being his own boss he joined some of the staff and bought an interest in a small trade journal called the *Western Lumberman* instead. With the children now old enough to take care of themselves, Margaret decided it was time to put her homesteading experience to good use too. After all, pioneering on the homestead helped build on her farming experience and plenty of new agrarian knowledge was added to what she'd learned in her childhood on the Kansas farm.

Margaret founded her own publication, calling it *Country Life in B.C.* From an office next door to George's, she began to churn out articles on everything from bee keeping to poultry marketing. In the Murray household, if dinner conversation wasn't about lumber it was about problems with aphids or some such farming dilemma. While Margaret's grammar hadn't improved, she had George's fast pencil to make sure the copy was correct. In addition, George regularly contributed articles of his own. Together they developed a seamless publishing partnership, both charging out over the countryside to gather news at the same time. George visited lumber mills. Margaret took in the joys of swine growers' picnics or bee keepers' conventions. The children weren't immune either. They were often stuffed in the back seat of the family motorcar and dragged along to farms and auctions as well.

Of Publishing and Politics

Life seemed to be turning out all right for the Murrays. As Margaret would often say it was "vergin' on the verge." But it never managed to get there. In 1928 the economy was sliding again and Margaret had to relinquish her glossy magazine, unable to attract advertisers. The *Western Lumberman* had the opposite problem. It was doing so well the majority owners decided to sell. Suddenly, the couple was out of work again.

The day George had to turn over his keys to the *Western Lumberman* office, he scooped up the last $10 in Margaret's purse and took H.R. MacMillan to lunch. MacMillan had received a subsidy from Ottawa to promote trade with Japan. At the time he had a small fleet that was shipping British Columbia lumber to the Far East. The fleet usually returned with cheaply manufactured dry goods, a proprietor's dream. George, still a believer in the glowing economic prospects of British Columbia, convinced MacMillan he could be exporting other B.C. products as well as lumber. MacMillan was interested and agreed to help pay for George to travel to the Orient so he could scout things out, and write some articles about the market there at the same time. Margaret, once again, offered a smile of encouragement to George.

Ever ready to support her husband, she had a few promotional ideas of her own.

Chapter 3
Life in Lillooet

Georege spent four months in the Orient writing his newspaper articles while exploring new export market potential for MacMillan's fleet. But additional Far East opportunities for MacMillan looked slim. In the meantime, forty of the Southam papers ran his dispatches from the Orient, paying George by the word.

While he was gone, Margaret revived a feature that had been popular with the women readers of *Country Life*. Rug hooking. She invested in hooks, canvas, wool, and bats, and with the children safely placed in a boarding school, toured the province teaching farmwives how to turn rags into rugs. Margaret, however, was not a prodigy in that fine art. The few rugs she made were foisted upon her in-laws, for a price of course, and few of the women she taught ever seemed to need a repeat lesson. Nevertheless, the venture did provide a meager income while she waited for George's articles to be published in Southam newspapers. She used rug-hooking profits to buy a cow, a pig, and some chickens for the homestead. Along with the garden she planted, Margaret established a self-sustaining farm operation just as the Great Depression began. Through the depression, the Murrays managed to survive at the homestead on what they could produce and on George's small salary.

When George returned from the Orient, before taking a job as a reporter on Southam's evening daily the *Vancouver Province*, he made a side trip to the Peace River country, an area which had been luring him since childhood.

Transportation of grain and beef from northern British Columbia to the coast continued to stymie George's solution to the problem of provincial prosperity. The government simply had to step in, he believed, and he said so to anyone who would listen. He had a ready audience in the political party he still supported. The homestead soon became a social centre for Liberal gatherings with as many as 30 people arriving for Sunday dinners. All were cooked and served by Margaret, country-style of course.

In 1933, the province was broke. The Murray guests believed the electorate was eager to see some change in government. George concluded it was time to get back into politics but that meant the Murrays would have to move. Securing a nomination in Vancouver would be next to impossible for a politician who eked an existence from a homestead in the scrub. Vancouver voters would want a candidate with the patina of prosperity, one who lived in the city. George decided his only chance was to be elected in a riding located over the mountains somewhere in the province's interior. He got party support to run in the south Cariboo district out of the rustic village of Lillooet.

Lillooet was 375 kilometres up the Fraser River from the coast. One of the largest communities in the province during the Cariboo Gold Rush, it had dwindled to the size of a hamlet. But that fact (potentially) made gaining a seat easier for an outsider. With the barest of belongings — little more than a frying pan, a butcher knife, and a feather bed — the couple headed east in their Willys Knight sedan. They had $200 in campaign funds, 3000 election blotters, a typewriter, and a case of whiskey. Sagebrush country had no idea what was about to descend.

Margaret learned first hand, with a white-knuckled grip on the dashboard, why it had taken the Royal Engineers four years to build the 150 kilometre road from Lytton to Lillooet. It was as if it the surveyors had followed the old pack trails once used to reach the community. From Lytton, where the Fraser and the Thompson Rivers meet — the road was a winding goat track with mountainside on the right — and the churning muddy Fraser far below on the left. During August, the Fraser Canyon became a natural oven with temperatures so high the heat shimmered in the air. Margaret prayed for deliverance as they chugged their way east along the road. She would have felt more comfortable in a horse-drawn buggy. Furtively, she whispered unwelcomed driving instructions to George as he navigated the tight curves along the narrow mountain road.

When they finally reached the village that was to become their home during the three-month election campaign, Margaret must have thought she'd driven back in time. For all appearances, Lillooet could have been a Wild West frontier town. An undulating wooden sidewalk, its planks heaved here and there, edged the main street. The buildings were a mix of Victorian gingerbread and boxy ship-lap. They showed the weathered gray look of age. The churches they passed were dilapidated evidence of absent prosperity.

Lillooet marked "Mile 0" on the Cariboo Road, the trail that led miners to the gold fields in 1858. The road began with Lillooet's Main Street. It was wide enough to turn a team of oxen without backing up and served regularly as a racetrack for spirited miners when they came into town. Margaret was sure the village looked much as it would have 75 years earlier when Lillooet had a transient population of 10,000 gold seekers. It didn't appear residents planned on renovations any time soon.

That night the Murrays climbed out their hotel window to a small balcony over the sidewalk outside the hotel saloon, and took in their surroundings. "Well, what do you think?" George asked.

"It sure as hell isn't much of a town," Margaret replied carefully. "But it's pretty. Has atmosphere." George was disappointed in her reaction.

Arm in arm, the couple took in the moonlight view of the Fraser and the almost phosphorescent glow of the glaciers on the mountain peaks high above the village. In the dim light, Lillooet assumed a different personality. Margaret playfully nudged her husband with her hip as they leaned on the railing. "Actually, I've never seen anything as beautiful."

Who knows where that romantic moment might had led if several drunks hadn't stumbled from the saloon, shouting and swinging at each other. They had chosen the ground directly outside the Murray's perch for a melee and Margaret exploded with Irish indignation. Ignoring George's pleas to let matters be, she reached through her window, and retrieved a china pitcher full of water. She poured the water on the drunks and demanded they go home so "decent folks" could get some sleep. With a few well-placed cuss words and a wet taste of the Lally temper, Margaret introduced herself to Lillooet.

In the weeks that followed, the brash character of the district's newest female resident became the talk in mining camps, saloons, and parlours from Pemberton to Bralorne. Margaret campaigned for George wherever voters were settled, using a folksy, down-to-earth approach that appealed to the hearty population of loners. In Bralorne particularly, she showed she was capable of matching wit and sarcasm with any comer.

George's stumping took him from one corner of the riding to the other. During the campaign he was constantly moving about on trains, autos, wagons, and by bush plane. When he was booked to speak to a gathering of miners in Bralorne, a mining town miles up the Bridge River from Lillooet, Margaret did the advance job. On that occasion her husband was due to speak at 8:00 p.m. But when he still hadn't arrived by 8:25 p.m.,

Margaret saw he was losing his crowd. She reluctantly took to the stage.

The room full of men made their disappointment obvious. There were a few catcalls and loud asides about her ample figure. Margaret, who had not had experience speaking to a crowd such as this, gritted her teeth. She apologized for George's tardy arrival and went through a bland recitation of his credentials. The miners showed their boredom by heckling and jeering and rapid-fire questions. What will George Murray do for prospectors? What about that road?

"If you boys will shut up and show me the common courtesy of listening, I may tell you," she shouted back. "My husband thinks that he has something to offer. He thinks he can save the people, but I tell him most of the people don't give a damn about being saved!" The miners started to laugh. Margaret continued, "He started his career as a cub reporter on the *Ottawa Journal* in 1908, waiting for his day. He used to tell me his hopes and dreams for this beloved province of his, and me with only the RC Catechism and Hale's Almanac for a background."

The men clapped. Her self-deprecating humility had struck a responsive cord. She continued, moving from one ribald story about her Kansas upbringing to another, bridging the comments with references to provincial government policies and how her husband would see things change. By the time his chartered bush plane skimmed to a stop on Gun Lake, the men were rapt and ready. George promised to build a road from Lillooet up the Yalakom River east of the Shulaps Range if he was elected. He promised grubstakes for prospectors. George had never had a better crowd.

For the rest of September Margaret relied on the lessons she learned that night. To her, travelling the hustings was like making the visits to the advertisers back in Collingwood. Half the time, all the voters wanted was a good listener and the other half a reason to argue. Not just about highways and unemployment either. They wanted to talk about how to cure the ailments of hogs, to share their dreams of marriage, to tell tales of their labour, and to share their triumphs and losses. They took Margaret's homespun approach either as a welcome dose of friendly humour or a bad case of bother, but they all took it just the same. And they remembered her. As she walked the Pacific Great Eastern Railway (PGE) tracks from Squamish to Shalath, Margaret asked for votes and all the while, made notes. The small black book she carried everywhere, wrapped shut with a sturdy band of elastic, contained these people's dreams and their stories, their recipes and their family trees. By the time of the election in the first days of October 1933, the

Murrays had made many friends and they could count each one by the X they marked on their ballots.

George won the election easily. Margaret, with her notebook closely guarded, was ready to start another newspaper.

When Margaret started the job of creating a newspaper in the tiny community of Lillooet she had no money and no backers. But she did have spunk. There was no end to the stories she and George could tap out after the election campaign if given half a chance and some advertising support. The couple was now aware of the region's colourful past and intimate with its present struggles. They also had their sights locked on what they saw as a great future for the valley.

In 1934, Lillooet was undergoing its seventh gold rush but most didn't care. Least of all the Chinese. Their ancestors had arrived a generation before, tried their hand at mining, and found safer employment as restaurant proprietors, vegetable importers, and laundry owners. They'd settled into the quiet routine of feeding the locals and stocking their pantries. The price of gold, though it was news on Vancouver's Howe Street, didn't raise a Chinese eyebrow. This gold rush was a stampede for the promoters, the speculators, and the mining companies. Regular folks were content to watch.

Their newspaper's coverage area reached out in a

wide circle with Lillooet at its centre. It went from Pemberton inland to Shalath and then Lillooet. It stretched to Lytton in one direction and up the Bridge River valley in the other, ending at the mining community of Gold Bridge. Margaret tried to explain the value of advertising to the small cadre of customers in Lillooet with hardly any success. Wo Hing bought a six-word ad, little more than the name of his store. At Jim Brothers the diminutive proprietor listened politely to the sales pitch, his abacus clicking as she told him the cost, and then shook his head. "Why advertise? Everyone knows we are on Main Street anyway," Mrs. Jim said, with matter-of-fact assurance. Margaret did find some success at Fred Hunt's store. This Chinese merchant (who had anglicized his name years before) bought a 30 cm ad space and became the biggest advertiser in the *Bridge River–Lillooet News*.

George had better luck selling ads in Gold Bridge. The Pioneer Mine and the Bralorne Mines in the Bridge River valley were booming and townsite boundaries were not yet defined. Entrepreneurs were setting up little businesses in tents and shacks as fast as they could find a piece of ground to settle. For George, the pickings were good, with ads easily sold to outfitters and restaurants and even to barbers.

Thanks to a group of married women in Gold

Bridge, who wanted to ban prostitution, the Murrays' newspaper success was assured. With the number of single men in the area, it didn't take long for enterprising prostitutes to establish 'sporting houses' among the quickly built structures. Three, in fact, were rising next door to what was soon to become St. Margaret's Church. Much to the consternation of the local padre, the busiest road in the area was the one leading to an already established brothel called Les Girls. The more pious women in his congregation wanted a stop put to the construction of any more brothels. The issue quickly began to split the community, dividing them along lines of revelry versus family values. The married women called for controls on the prostitution and had the School Board on their side. The board claimed that the customers' vehicles created a traffic hazard for school children across the road from Les Girls. The Board of Trade in Gold Bridge was more willing to look blindly at the sprouting "houses of ill repute." And businessmen saw the brothels as good for commerce generally.

A major portion of Gold Bridge's population was single men, with 500 to 600 miners living in bunkhouses and tents in the valley. Thus, Margaret defended the "girls" in her paper. "They were here first," she editorialized. "If you want them to move, let's get in and help them move. Allow them uptown on mail days to shop. Stop harassing them. After all, Gold Bridge was happy enough to sell them lots and lumber for their houses. They don't bother anybody. And it's fine to adjust your rose-coloured glasses and say these houses shouldn't exist. But until 600 single men in this valley can build themselves homes and bring wives and families here, you may as well relax and face the fact that sporting houses are necessary to the safety of the women who do live here."

Her stand wasn't too popular with the women's leagues of the churches, but Margaret didn't care. She had the solid support of the miners.

With George often away representing his constituents in Victoria, Margaret had a free hand publishing her lurid prose filled with grammatical errors and malapropisms. She covered accidents, inquests, trials, and socials with the same folksy outspoken style. Always blatantly personal and thoroughly opinionated, she drew reader criticism as often as she did reader encouragement. She was proud of every vilifying letter to the editor she received. "Shows they're reading my pars" (Margaret's jargon for paragraphs) she told the children. Margaret insisted on publishing every scrap of correspondence the paper received in the Letters to the Editor (opposite her editorials) whether the reader called her names or not.

The *Bridge River–Lillooet News* was produced at Mitchell Press in Vancouver for two years before the Murrays established their own shop in Lillooet. Their first staffer was 19-year-old Georgina, fresh from schooling in California where she got a "civilized upbringing" under the prim guidance of Margaret's sisters.

While her younger brother Dan had spent most of his teen years in Vancouver at private schools, Georgie had passed most of hers under the care of her father's family. She had been treated to an education in music by a father who dreamed of her becoming a concert pianist, though it was not something Georgina put on her own agenda. She ended her teens at school in San Francisco for a year. She even spent time working as kitchen help in Oakland, a tour of duty Margaret totally supported as the topper to her daughter's education.

At the paper, Georgie aimed high. With copies of *Time* magazine, *Wall Street Journal*, *New York Times*, and (the former Maclean–Hunter's) *Mayfair Magazine* as her templates, she began writing for the newspaper as if it were being read in the capitals of the world rather than the privies of Gold Bridge. Even the social news became high society copy under Georgie's hand, but Margaret soon put an end to that. "I absolutely defy Mr. Timothy Eaton to recognize the outfit you put on that girl," Margaret chastised on one occasion when Georgie turned in her report on a wedding. "I saw that wedding party as they were going into the beer parlor on the way to the ceremony. A cathedral veil? It looked more like a net curtain to me. And where did you get the organ music? They played her in on an accordion." Unfortunately, Margaret couldn't be hanging over Georgie's shoulder and writing copy in Gold Bridge at the same time.

Another of Georgie's tasks was proofreading and she learned that the hard way too. An ad for Vaughan Dubois' garage and taxi service proclaimed Dubois had the best and most reliable *tool* in the Bridge River Valley. For some reason the *s* in the word tools had mysteriously disappeared. Dubois pulled his advertising. Jimmy Pollard, a respected Howe Street stockbroker had opened a sub-office at Pioneer Mines. The report that passed through Georgie's proofreading claimed, "*Storks* are moving fast, and Jimmy Pollard is getting the lion's share of all the business." Pollard pulled his advertising. The report on a mining accident was even more embarrassing. This time it was an *f* that went missing. The report should have read; "Ollie had just finished two hours of his afternoon *shift*, when the door of the cage came unfastened and fell on his foot, breaking it in several places." Ollie moved to Ontario.

Via an imperfect phone connection, Margaret rained down her fury on her daughter, even though the girl was trying her best to get the paper produced on her own 170 miles away.

"I really am sorry, Mother."

"You'll be sorry when your carelessness loses us every ad in this paper," Margaret shouted. "And what about applesauce at the school concert? That's almost as bad. In fact it's worse."

"Applesauce? I don't remember anything about applesauce at the school concert."

"You wool-gatherer, you! It was applause…a-p-p-l-a-u-s-e…children reciting…school concert! And you made it applesauce. The mothers are furious."

But the litany of errors had a bright side. Copies of those papers sold for as much as five dollars each.

The *News* was always ready and willing to voice unpopular views if it was in support of better conditions in the mines or if it prompted the area's economic prosperity. The paper was as accurate a gauge of voter opinion as any high-priced survey because the letters written by the public complimented George as often as they railed at Margaret. He was re-elected to a second term in 1937. One of the reasons was his campaign for workplace improvements at the mines, which was featured prominently in the pages of the *Bridge River–Lillooet News.*

The men working underground were close to George's heart. Consumption was an occupational disease, so George authored the first plan in British Columbia to compensate stricken miners. The mining companies, however, were convinced many of the victims had contracted the disease in other provinces. Although the result of his efforts meant a complete disappearance of mining company advertising in the *News*, he pushed legislation that forced a nine percent tax levy on the mining industry to pay silicotic miners.

The mining companies pulled their advertising from the small news-sheet once more when the paper loudly supported a workers' strike. Again, that didn't change the stance of the MLA and his wife. But sometimes their goal to be the voice of the community went a little too far.

The paper faithfully published guest registers of local hotels with as much seriousness as the Police Blotter. Margaret's intent was to inform her business readers of the comings and goings of important or notable businessmen. However, when a Vancouver lawyer requested a back issue for use as evidence in a divorce proceeding, Margaret put an end to that practice.

Usually the Murrays relied on the mail to deliver the week's news to Mitchell Press. Or the telegraph for late-breaking news. On occasion however, Margaret climbed aboard the PGE to deliver the copy by hand when something special had to be added. "I got a coupl'a pars here to write," Margaret would announce at the front counter and then describe what had to be added. Usually her descriptions kept the office staff in rapt attention. Though the happenings were of little importance in their lives, her colourful reporting could turn the simplest incident into a fascinating account. A landslide at Ogden was a good example.

Margaret described the news of the slide from the local dentist's point-of-view. "Our travelling dentist, Dr. Lowe, had this plate grinning in his hand, its owner in the chair. He was shooting the breeze, when 'BOOM' the mountain started to slide. Well sir, the folks around Ogden didn't know whether Doc had drilled right through his patient, the floor, and the mountain side or whether he'd changed bits and was practicing for the miner's hand drilling contest.... They sent a search party after the plate and found it down on the Native Son property. And according to what I hear, the gold in that plate may be the only gold Native Son will ever see around there...."

When the Murrays finally had equipment installed in Lillooet to produce the paper locally, it was running an average of six to eight pages. Getting the weekly paper out themselves would require all the staff positions that Mitchell Press had provided, such as compositors to set the type with the hot-lead linotype machines. They also needed a printer to put that type into forms and to operate the press. Their shop on Lillooet's Main Street was in a building that had been abandoned for years. Originally a boarding house (raised in 1912 for railway construction workers) it was big, ugly, and tired. Its space, chopped up by 10 tiny cubicles on the upper floor, had once housed an illegal nightclub, with a Chinese restaurant below. It came with 40 hectares of hillside, a log barn that had housed camels (used as pack animals during the Cariboo gold rush), and a dilapidated garage. It had no indoor plumbing. The Murrays thought it was perfect for the paper.

The lobby was large enough for an antique hand-turned press. The old nightclub dance floor became home to the linotype (used to form the newspaper type from a cauldron of molten lead) and a workbench became the form table (where the type was pieced together). A lawyer named P.J. Wilson, who also used the building for his office, was taken in as a boarder. Ling, a Chinese cook, was hired to feed everyone out of the old restaurant kitchen. And the Murrays moved in upstairs.

Cubicle No. 5, down the hall from Margaret's bedroom, was selected as the editorial office. They outfitted it with two homemade kitchen tables, a swivel chair, a clunky Underwood typewriter, and a telephone. Through a hole cut into the floor, a string served to pass copy to the linotype operator, and a length of garden hose fitted with funnels at either end became the *Bridge River–Lillooet News* intercom system.

George's hiring style relied more on gut instinct than resumes. Their first compositor, an 18-year-old with a spine deformity, was hired from a car wash in Vancouver because George felt "he could stand some of this good Lillooet sunshine." The pressroom staff ran the gambit, from "tramp" printers who often had alcohol problems, to the mentally disturbed. Despite their personal problems, every wandering printer the Murrays hired got a helping hand through the *News*. A printer George had found (in the PGE gas car rolling towards Lillooet from Shalath) snapped one day and began goose-stepping around the press. Margaret decided it was time for some stability. Time to introduce their son, 17-year-old Dan Murray to the business. She wangled him training with the *North Shore Press*, a newspaper in Vancouver, and within weeks he was handling the linotype with ease.

Many of the printers they hired had worked with the best writers of the day, and Dusty (Warnock) Medford was among the finest. Over the years he'd worked at many of Canada's largest newspapers. Dusty regularly organized the layout of the *News* to mimic the various styles other papers had adopted. While interesting, it gave the paper a curious style that changed according to whatever copy dropped from the ceiling on clothespins.

Dusty was usually able to adapt to the unexpected. He could handle most anything, even tight deadline calamities that might have stopped other printers and compositors dead. But on one occasion, when the linotype refused to drop its *t*s, Dusty came unglued. He cussed and fumed and began taking his frustration out on the linotype with a ball peen hammer.

"What's all that racket?" George shouted from the editorial office.

"We're sunk," Dusty replied with a yell into his funnel. "A half column of your editorial can't be set, George. My *t*s aren't droppin' for Chrissakes."

George calmly told Dusty to grab a cup of Ling's coffee and relax. A half-hour later he'd rewritten the editorial without using a single *t*. The feat stunned Dusty, who promptly traded coffee for something stronger and spent the rest of the day in the beer parlor.

Such feats of journalistic excellence were commonplace with George. Had it been Margaret at the other end of the funnel of course, having no *t*s wouldn't have mattered. She would have pushed the newspaper out the door anyway and simply told readers to add the letter themselves.

Margaret was a public relations expert long before Madison Avenue coined the term. Dealing with the press and advertisers came as naturally to her as talking. Margaret knew you had to get a prospect's attention and did so with fresh slabs of bacon, boxes of gold-bearing quartz, and bags of vegetables from her garden. Margaret regularly ventured into Vancouver to peddle the value of her little paper to the executives of companies that ought to be advertising — or to editors of the daily newspapers who ought to be telling the world how good a read the *News* really was — even for subscribers on the mainland of British Columbia.

George and Margaret were on just such a sales trip in Vancouver about a year after starting the *News* and, as was their custom, they stayed at the Georgia Hotel. Margaret came loaded down with harvest booty including two fat, plucked, and ready-to-roast turkeys. As they registered, a deskman unfamiliar with the couple asked if twin beds were preferred. "Young man," Margaret boomed, "we want a double bed. We're old-fashioned people. If people used double beds more there would be less trouble in the world today. Save your twin beds for a gal you can see daylight through her withers."

An embarrassed George hustled Margaret into the

elevator to escape the stares and snickers of other guests in the lobby who had overheard, but the memorable visit didn't end with the doors swooshing shut. Because the couple had arrived too late to store the turkeys overnight in the hotel restaurant's freezer, Margaret had to devise a different means of preservation. What she came up with was homespun and practical. With twine, she tied the necks together, anchored the birds to the radiator, and dropped them out the window. As dawn arrived, so did a flock of seagulls making such a loud fuss over this tantalizing meal that their screeches woke up all the guests on the north side of the hotel. Margaret was nonplussed. The turkeys had kept overnight in the chilly Vancouver air with only a few pecks on the flesh as evidence.

Chapter 4
Death and Destruction in Shanghai

I n July 1937, George had four months during the Legislative Assembly's summer break in which he could beat the drum for his pet project, boosting B.C. trade. As the couple was in Victoria when the legislature's session ended, the children back in Lillooet were told not to expect mother and father home anytime soon. With little more than a phone call's notice, Margaret and George boarded a Canadian Pacific steamship, the *Empress of Asia*, and headed to China.

In the four months the Murrays were in China, Margaret filed 55 full newspaper columns of copy for the *Bridge River–Lillooet News*. Each column of 52 centimetres contained almost 2000 words. Her reports could have formed a healthy-sized novel. She wrote to her faithful readers in Lillooet about the people and the places, the events and the hardships. And she described the circumstances that nearly led to their deaths on two different occasions. Margaret took her readers on every step of the journey from Vancouver, sailing with them up the Wangpoo (Huangpu) River into the mysterious world of Shanghai.

Situated on the East China Sea, Shanghai was actually two cities in the 1930s. The Chinese outer city (the Chinese City) and a foreign inner city (the International Settlement). The latter was an insular hub of commerce with banks, embassies, and hotels just beyond the Bund (the central waterfront). For western travellers, reaching the Bund from the harbour meant crossing the humanity-clogged streets of the outer city with all its foreign smells and sights.

Margaret's first view of Shanghai and the Bund came amid the water-going chaos teeming along the docks where their steamship had berthed. A bobbing carpet of boats skimmed over the harbour between British and American warships. These foreign vessels were stationed there to protect their nationals.

In July 1937, the second Sino-Japanese war had

broken out. Japan had been facing severe economic depression since 1920. The growth of its population was far outstripping an ability to cope economically. In an attempt to counter a lack of natural resources and foreign markets, Japan had adopted a military expansionist policy that included an attempt to assume control over China. The Japanese army already had a stranglehold on Manchuria but until July, fighting with China had been sporadic. Nationalist Chinese army units were plagued by a lack of supplies, poor training, and corrupt leadership. When Japanese units were attacked at the Marco Polo Bridge outside of Peking (Beijing), however, vicious fighting broke out and quickly raged throughout western China. Japanese troops moved with haste to seize major coastal cities and much of the countryside. The fear of war prompted more than a million Chinese refugees to flood into the International City of Shanghai for safety — just as the Murrays arrived.

Shanghai was in dangerous state of flux as the couple prepared to enter the city. Margaret noted that the western warships were steaming further up the river only to be replaced by six Japanese versions. She marvelled at the junks zigzagging in the path of the steel ships, the fearful eyes painted on their bows somehow guiding them through the confusion of sampans, barges, and small water taxis. From the upper deck of their steamship she could also see the tall needle of the Meteorological Tower at the dock, its pagoda-like cap dressed in nautical flags. She didn't know it was visually broadcasting the state of the weather to anyone familiar with the language of triangles and diamonds. The tower, like everything else, was part of an overwhelming vista of strangeness to the Kansas farm girl.

Their hotel was the Cathay, an over-the-top accommodation that British and American foreigners had insisted on erecting. Perhaps a sign of their superiority in that place of squalor, it offered guests a private plumbing system fed by a spring on the outskirts of town, marble baths with silver taps, and lavatories imported from Britain. Just being in the building made Margaret uncomfortable and uneasy as she thought of the raw poverty in the Chinese City. The Cathay was expensive and the staff were haughty. It seemed insulated from the real Shanghai. Being separated from the action didn't sit well with Margaret.

The Japanese Emperor's flagship the *Idzuma*, serving duty as the temporary Japanese Consulate, was already berthed on the river within sight of the Cathay. That night Margaret and George went to the Park Hotel for dinner and dancing and listened to the strange sound of explosions as the Chinese scuttled junks on a river sandbar to prevent the easy entrance of any more

Japanese vessels than were already dotting the harbour. While they dined, Margaret learned that two Japanese officers had been killed during the afternoon. The troops, the warships, and the killings had put Chinese Shanghai in turmoil. But to Margaret's amazement the foreign nationals on the dance floor at the Park Hotel were barely concerned about the little "boom boom" underway.

"Endless refugees pass below our window," she later wrote to the *News* before climbing into bed. "Rather dignified lot with their household treasures, mostly clocks, in their arms. We will look for another hotel." It took a day for them to settle in, book the passage they would need later to leave Shanghai for Singapore, and to find a new hotel. Their transfer couldn't come soon enough for Margaret. "Dinner tonight cost a dollar more than last night," she complained in her next report. "What a joke this all is. No business can be transacted. George can't leave the settlement area until this is settled. We could see burning territory in three directions last night from the 32nd floor of the Park Hotel where we danced a little and pretended not to be alarmed."

On their third morning in the city, while riding the elevator down to the lobby, Margaret traded impressions of Shanghai and the brewing conflict with Eleanor

Roosevelt. The Murrays had decided to move to a less expensive hotel called the Metropole. Hefting her bags while George settled accounts at the front desk, Margaret watched a train of porters handling luggage for the U.S. president's wife. Polite navy officers were carefully escorting Eleanor away from the danger. Margaret secretly wished she could go along.

She put on her now patented brave-face-smile for George. But once they'd moved to their new digs, a few blocks from the Cathay, she described her day more honestly. "Our room has a terrace overlooking the harbour. The refugees are swarming in. Different from yesterday. Riding, running, rickshaw, wheelbarrow, coolie, motor, walking, crawling, they descend, clawing and fighting their way through the traffic. The alleyways are glutted. Where they won't be trampled to death, they will sink to the dirty street and fall asleep. I tipped that sheik at the door to let the poor woman rest on the step. She wasn't resting, she was squatting to give birth. He threatened her with his bamboo lily and she crawled around the corner. Mother of God, what is happening?"

That afternoon there was no question a war had broken out in Shanghai. The Japanese Emperor's flagship the *Idzuma* was berthed on the river at the Nippon Yusen Kaisha Wharf, within sight of the Cathay. Two Chinese warplanes dropped through heavy cloud cover, intent on destroying the Japanese ship, but instead their bombs fell off target. One dropped into the river not far from the Bund, opposite the Shanghai Club. Another hit the wharf beyond the ship. Then again, at 4:30 p.m., three more Chinese bombers came screaming over the International Settlement from west to east. Amid heavy anti-aircraft fire the pilot of the lead plane dropped his bombs, this time errantly hitting the Palace Hotel and demolishing its upper storeys. Another bomb fell between the Palace Hotel and the Cathay in the midst of thousands of Chinese refugees swarming in the streets. One of the other planes, apparently damaged by the defensive fire, dropped its load of bombs over the most crowded corner in Shanghai. The two explosives fell almost at the centre of the junction between Tibet Road and Avenue Edward VII. One exploded on impact and the other in mid-air just a few metres above ground. The result was a savage scene of slaughter. Thousands of people torn to pieces by the blast in a split second.

As the Chinese planes swooped over the city and dropped their bombs, Margaret counted 21 Japanese ships in the harbour, all shooting in defense. The stench of cordite was almost as sickening to her as the odour of human excreta wafting up to the terrace from the street below. Suddenly, their plan to slip from Shanghai to Singapore was no longer a future one. George decided an immediate departure was prudent and got Margaret to promise she would stay in the room while he tried to hasten arrangements for their departure. Margaret closed the window to the terrace and pulled the drapes, trying to insulate herself from the fear outside. For comfort she continued to write about what was happening in case they weren't lucky enough to escape the chaos quickly. When George returned, his news wasn't good.

"George is back to change his shoes," she reported. "He is white and sick and carrying one shoe, covered with bloody foam and tissue. He slipped off a fallen slate outside and into a human chest cavity."

"Darkness is falling. Heavenly Father, what a holocaust. The asphalt caught fire and is burning paint, blood, entrails. The smell. Awful. Cars upside down. Fifty killed this afternoon at the Cathay," she wrote, overlooking the obvious luck they'd had not to be counted among the dead.

The next day the *Idzuma* moved further from the front harbour and a lull in the fighting was the welcome result. George again took advantage, trying to find the steamship office on Nanking Road (Nanjing Road) where he'd made his cheap-rate booking to Kowloon the day they'd arrived. When he got there however, he found six dead Chinese, piled like cordwood on either side of the doorway.

Ma Murray

The Murrays had arrived in Shanghai intending to use a letter of credit for their expenses, but the sudden outbreak of hostility had made cash the only way to get action for even the smallest service. Shanghai dollars were impossible to get as the banks had closed and bank employees were scrambling to move to safer locations. George and Margaret found themselves in serious jeopardy and out of cash. But on the trek back to the Metropole, George had another idea. The British warship was disembarking its soldiers and was scheduled to leave by noon. "If we can get to the harbour, we can board a lighter (a flat bottomed barge used for loading and unloading ships) which will take us out to the ship," George said excitedly when Margaret was back in his arms. "There'll be climbing. Can you do it? We have less than an hour." He began to stuff papers into his briefcase. Margaret emptied the dresser drawers, ignoring the clothes they'd hung in the closet and her beloved typewriter as she rushed to pack as many essentials as she could carry. Then George groaned....

There were rickshaws waiting to take hotel guests outside and he realized he had no money to pay the driver. Not even a dime. He feverishly fingered every pocket in every hanging garment, but not a stray coin could be found. Margaret sat on the bed to call upon the help of St. Anthony and suddenly remembered

Lillooet...she'd been mending and she'd slipped a fifty-cent piece into her sewing kit for the iceman but he'd never arrived.... With a wink and a loud exclamation, she revealed it to her husband and then stuffed it, with some pixies, into his pocket.

George was still exclaiming his good fortune at having married Irish luck as the rickshaw driver skidded on the slippery streets towards the berths in the harbour. He'd already given the boy the money, but unless the driver ran full out, George knew they might not make it to the ship in time. Margaret saw him patting his pocket as he urged the driver on through the crowds. When they arrived at the dock, their driver was too exhausted to help with their bags. The Murrays tumbled aboard the lighter that was to carry them to the HMS *Falmouth* along with a score of foreigners, none of whom discounted the "little boom boom" any longer. They had made it with only a few minutes to spare.

To their amazement, as they scrambled over the benches of the heaving boat to reach the warship's makeshift gangway minutes later, they heard their names being called over the ship's loud hailer. "Will the premier of British Columbia and Mrs. Murray please come to the bridge...."

George was already climbing the gangway. He stopped to look back at Margaret and when he did he patted his pocket once again. The British Navy had mistaken their guests. Neither George nor Margaret rushed to clarify their identity. Protocol meant that as "distinguished guests," instead of making their journey to Kowloon beside the stretchers and ill refugees in an evil-smelling windowless hold, they would have the relative comfort of a private cabin.

"We can't stay here," Margaret whispered to George once they were shown to the executive officer's quarters that had been hastily reserved for them. "Those stretcher cases. The children. This…luxury…this space?"

"I may not be premier of British Columbia, but it's our cabin," George adamantly replied.

Though Margaret agreed to sleep there, she didn't hide away. That night she helped tend to the sick and the fearful in the Executive Officers' Lounge, and assisted another fleeing navy guest through childbirth. For the first time since she'd left Canada, Margaret felt right at home.

Chapter 5
The Call of the North

Back in Lillooet, Georgina and Dan did their best to maintain a positive bank balance at the *Bridge River–Lillooet News*. Margaret's reports had continued to arrive by mail, but out of sequence, and many weeks after they had been written. It didn't worry the young newspaper marvels. They'd get around to publishing the reports when they had the order right, and besides, there were so many other things to consider. Like starting another newspaper.

In an inspired flash of brilliance, editor Georgina had decided that a newspaper to compete with the

Williams Lake Tribune (in ranching country farther up the PGE line) made complete sense. She convinced her brother of her acumen and together the two Murray children took to the road with advance copies of the *Cariboo News*. By huckstering in a carnival booth at the Williams Lake Rodeo, they managed to sell 27 subscriptions (with promise of as many more to come) and vigorously complimented each other on their accomplishment.

They learned quickly however, that it took more than a flash of newness to secure the confidence of a readership. In the weeks that followed the bills for printing began to pile up, eating away at the meager profit the Lillooet paper had managed to build. They struggled to sell advertising at a distance and welcomed subscriptions in the hope of receiving payment sometime in the future. The foolishness of their endeavour started to gnaw at them, especially when they remembered that sooner or later they'd have to show their books to a not very kindly publisher who had an extremely sharp tongue.

When the *Vancouver Province* contacted Georgie by telephone soon after their creative newspaper launch, asking if she'd heard from her mother, Georgie felt wretched. No news had been received about Margaret or George for three weeks, the news reporter told her. They appeared to be unreported somewhere in the Pacific, but the caller added, hopefully, "The Red Cross will keep checking — so no real worry — yet." A cloud of gloom descended over Georgie that didn't lift for two weeks.

"You've been getting out a not-bad paper," Margaret allowed after she and George reappeared at the *News* office unannounced and laden with packages and baggage. "You're not ready to be syndicated, but generally not bad," she told Georgie.

She gave her daughter a ticket to eastern Canada as reward and payment for months of unpaid work. Then promptly ordered Dan to go to Williams Lake with instructions not to return until he'd collected for "every damn sub sold" for the *Cariboo News*. Margaret was practical to a fault. Don't worry about the Lillooet paper, she told her children. "I'm home and I'm here to stay for the rest of my life!" Luckily for British Columbia that was not the way things evolved.

While George travelled across the country and into the United States on speaking engagements about Pacific trade, Margaret also saw some value in expanding the Lillooet publishing empire. Even though she thought the children's scheme for Williams Lake was a loser, she herself started another paper in Squamish. The *Howe Sound News* was created to promote George's vision for a seaport on Howe Sound to facilitate export. In it he predicted a harbour filled with grain ships and oil tankers, fed by trains loaded with Peace River products. Though the laughter didn't die down for years, George was eventually proven correct.

As the momentum for an impending world war built in Europe in 1939, the Murrays received an invitation to meet and be presented to King George VI and Queen Elizabeth of England, who were on a tour of the Dominion of Canada.

Margaret discussed the matter with her readers. What should I wear? What should I say? Answers came in fast and in large numbers, to the point where Margaret gave up trying to buy the proper dress or the appropriate hat or the perfect fox stole. Instead, she hopped in the car and drove to Vancouver where the Hudson's Bay store provided two boxes of blue wool. She had decided to knit her own outfit. After all, she had done it before. That time the wool never left her hands from the sheep to the dresser drawer — except for a bath in a mixture of horse urine, golden rod — and some Oregon grape root for colour.

While they waited in the anteroom to the Legislative Chamber for their audience, George fussed. It wasn't the prospect of meeting the king that got him nervous, it was worrying about what Margaret might do or say. Her Irish father, Pat Lally, held no love for the British and George knew his wife had been bred with some of that dislike. Would she pull the king from the dais and pound on him or (worse) give him a taste of Lally sentiment with her acid tongue? Or would she reach out and hug the regent, covering him with kisses in gratitude for his navy's rescue in Shanghai?

George stayed close, ready to interrupt either rash alternative. After the audience, Margaret described the event for the same readers who had actively offered their advice. "I didn't kiss him," she wrote, "but I shook hands till his poor little sword rattled." That was Margaret.

Meanwhile, in Europe, Germany had been readying for war. On September 1, 1939, Hitler's troops marched into Poland to set off a powder keg of global proportions. Within two days of Germany's invasion, the countries of Britain, France, Australia, New Zealand, India, and South Africa retaliated by declaring war on Germany. Canada added her name to the Allies, who pledged to fight against the Third Reich war machine, on September 10th.

The travesty abroad hit Margaret hard because Dan promptly enlisted in the army in spite of her pleas. To top it off the Pioneer Mines workers decided to strike in October. Because of the war, the strike was deemed to be illegal and Margaret stood firmly in support of the law. In a matter of weeks the miners, disgruntled at her editorial stand, cancelled their subscriptions. Those who agreed with her position joined the army. As a result the paper was left drifting, without much local support.

But that didn't stop her from speaking out. She turned instead to the provincial government, railing at George's boss (the premier) in her editorials. She complained about the state of the province's educational system, the roads, and the leadership Premier Pattullo was giving. Perhaps realizing it might cause a few ruffled feathers in the legislature, Margaret included a disclaimer at the bottom of the editorial. "No one else in the family or on the staff should be held responsible for this week's opinion. It's all mine. MLM."

That didn't help George's situation in Victoria. The Liberal government was fading under the pressure of the opposition and was considering a coalition government. George had been speaking against it, telling the other Liberal members it would be the end of the party in the province. Margaret's editorials only made it harder for George to find a friendly ear. As the 1939 provincial election approached, George took to writing editorials that predicted dire results for the Liberals instead of actively campaigning to hold his seat. The reader response was dramatic and negative. More cancelled subscriptions.

Margaret was fit to be tied. It was not her nature to give up and she couldn't stomach it in her husband. When Georgie wrote to tell her she was going to England with the WACS, Margaret's reply was pointed and angry. "I could fairly explode, shower brimstone and lava over a large area, burn some, and scare hell out of others. Your father takes so much time and management with his temperamental whims that this place has been disorganized since May 1. If he's licked in this election, he'll be like the peacock. And he will be licked unless he gums his hands to the task." George was soundly defeated.

After the election the federal government decided it would be safer for British Columbians if all residents of Japanese origin and their descendents were interned in special camps. It didn't matter to the government that the people they interned were Canadian citizens. Pearl Harbour was a burning memory and British Columbia had a long, scarcely defended coastline. If citizens had Japanese heritage they were a risk to security.

Margaret and George had been vocal in their fear of the Japanese after their experience in China, publicly supporting a careful watch on anyone of Japanese origin. They repeatedly warned their readers of the hidden menace (the very presence of Japanese Canadians) while Canada was at war. It was a racist stance. Without question.

Lillooet received 3800 Japanese, housing them in spartan quarters on its remote benches above the Fraser River. In spite of Margaret's screaming editorials, the local population in Lillooet accepted these new residents for the likeable and industrious people they were. Cash registers, dry from lack of use, starting ringing again. Even the Chinese softened to the new faces in their midst. And the community turned further away from the Murrays.

"You better look out, Margaret Murray, or the people around here will tar and feather you. And don't laugh. You hear some pretty heated talk standing behind those barroom taps," Jack Wright, the hotel operator warned.

"Ah, the hell with them," was Margaret's reply. "At least I'm honest and say what I think out in the open."

"That's all very well, but as a friend I'm warning you. Shut your mouth down there at that paper or leave town."

It all made Margaret feel very weary. Pushing an arthritically gnarled hand through her short salt-and-pepper hair, she spoke of this, and other warnings, with her husband of 27 years. Maybe the best medicine was a short reprieve from Lillooet, George suggested. The

Women's Institute was holding a convention in Regina and they'd sent her a ticket and money for expenses. Margaret agreed. It was another synchronistic event, she would say, that the Heavenly Father planted, for anyone attentive enough to notice.

While passing through the rail yards in Edmonton, Margaret saw a hurly-burly snarl of highway building equipment. "Where is that going?" she asked. "Up to the north," came a reply. Apparently, the highway equipment was being sent by the Americans to build a road.

It was George's road! The road to the north he'd been calling out to see built for nearly 30 years. The image of the Edmonton rail yard pestered her for the rest of the trip to Regina, and once she got there she decided she had to go back to find out more. She took in the convention's opening banquet, checked out of her hotel room, and boarded the train for Edmonton the same night.

In Edmonton she finagled a press pass from Northern Alberta Railways to take her to Dawson Creek. There were 17 sleeper coaches hooked up on that train carrying 480 people northward. Margaret learned it was only one of seven such trains that headed out from Edmonton that day. Each coach was packed with army officers, enlisted men, civilian road-building labourers, and even a few women. Twenty-four kilometres from

Dawson Creek Margaret saw an unbelievable depot. Solid stacks of lumber — buildings in pieces with doors and windows piled in bundles — bricks, blocks, and bales.

And Dawson Creek was even more frenzied. It teemed with uniforms. When Margaret tried to get a room at the Dew Drop Inn, she was told she was welcome to sit on a chair among 30 others who were also sitting on chairs, waiting for rooms.

After hitching a ride from Dawson Creek to Fort St. John she realized the real centre of all the activity was the tiny community (formerly tiny that is) of Fort St. John. The United States Army had built a camp three blocks west of town. It had hundreds of barracks and its own hospital and administration offices. Margaret stood on the dusty street with her mouth open, too stunned for words, counting tractors and trucks kicking up dust and spewing blue exhaust.

George had been preaching for half his life about the wealth to be tapped if only transportation could be pushed north. In 1931, after his first visit to China (to write articles on the trade potentials between British Columbia and the Asia-Pacific) he had visited the distant banks of the Peace River. He had told people down south that he'd gotten lost walking in fields that had wheat growing over his head. His was a gospel of reality but it seemed his only believer was Margaret.

The settlement of Fort St. John first grew around a fur-trading post. There was a log cabin hotel, a telegraph office, a general store, and a hospital. It was the centre of a land occupied by Natives and Europeans who trapped a country too bountiful to describe. For a long time the area was sparsely populated. But when furs were no longer the major industry, the settlers began to arrive. The Great Depression pulled them over impassable roads from the south to reach a place that could sustain and nourish them. Everyone in the north Peace country farmed, just to survive. There were few rules but those of nature by which to live. Life was simple and hard.

Until Grant McConachie decided to establish United Air Transport in Fort St. John, getting to the place was almost as hard as leaving it. Even after a proper air-field was established for the bush-flying outfit in 1940, it was difficult to reach. Flying in from Prince George took five days (the time needed to change from one kind of aircraft to another capable of landing in the soft north Peace earth when it wasn't frozen).

Then, on March 9, 1942 it all began to change. The Alcan Project was born and the U.S. Army arrived in the form of 10,000 troops and a procession of hissing, thumping, and grinding equipment. The road behe-moths they brought with them began to move in

Dawson Creek and never really stopped until they reached Fairbanks, Alaska.

When the Alcan Project was undertaken in March, the United States had only been at war for a few months and the Japanese were camped in the Aleutian Islands. An overland road link between Alaska and the lower 48 states had been studied as early as 1930 but it wasn't until the bombing of Pearl Harbour in December of 1941 that construction of the highway was deemed a defensive necessity. The general route was along a line of existing airfields from Edmonton, Alberta to Fairbanks, Alaska. Known as the Northwest Staging Route it was used to ferry more than 8000 war planes from Great Falls, Montana to Ladd Air Base in Fairbanks.

Before Margaret made her remarkable discovery of the goings on at Fort St. John, not a word had leaked south about the ambitious plan to build the road to Alaska. She was completely overwhelmed when she encountered all the equipment which was battling forest and muck in and around Fort St. John. By August, a trail had been cut — from Mile 0, the end of the wagon road from Dawson — all the way to Whitehorse. In the time that took, Fort St. John had changed from a one-restaurant hamlet to a thriving town with seven eateries.

On Margaret's initial walking tour of Fort St. John, she found the Canadian Bank of Commerce stuffed in the front of a garage because its own building had not yet arrived. A little distance away she saw an elaborate skeleton of scaffolding. This building (seemingly) was being raised right above the sleeping bags of its workers, who had to kip down each night on the floor. Everywhere she looked there was more of the same. Bakeries and theatres, hotels and dance halls, all in one stage or another of construction. Everything seemed to be half built, or waiting on workers.

It was like dreaming of a table loaded with food after suffering privation. Margaret was excited. More excited than she had ever been in her life. Her heart was pounding a tattoo. "George," she said to herself, "we're moving to Fort St. John."

It would take Margaret and George nearly a year to organize their lives in such a way that would allow them to move north. They'd been producing a meager paper since they had decided to print it in Vancouver for the duration of the war. The *Howe Sound News* became even smaller and the *Cariboo News* had been dropped from the books entirely. By the time the couple was ready to head for Fort St. John, they were barely able to pay their printing bills.

Georgie, in the meantime, had gone on to work for the CBC in Toronto. Margaret tried but couldn't convince her daughter to come home to help run the ailing family business. Dan was no help either. He had been away for four years already and was only coming back to Canada long enough to switch his sergeant's stripes for officer's pips. Again, Margaret pleaded with Georgie but to no avail. Georgina had inherited her mother's will but had learned to maintain a calm exterior, just as her father had always done when faced with her mother's volatile Irish temper. Georgie felt a stronger duty calling than the family newspapers. Instead of coming home, the young one-time editor (now broadcaster) decided to become a Wren SD (Special Duty), a writer with the Women's Branch of the Royal Canadian Navy in England.

"In the name of God what special duties are more important than this family's?" Margaret wrote her daughter when she learned of Georgie's decision. "The grapes of wrath will puck and bitter the lives of those who have a duty, who fail to ask God to aware them of it, who let someone else be an unworthy substitute."

At this point the Murrays had nothing to lose and everything to gain. So George, now 56 years old, got a pass on the Alaska Highway and headed north to have another look at the situation there, while Margaret (now age 55) stayed home to watch over the operations in Lillooet, Squamish, and Vancouver. When George returned a month later he was a changed man. He had

Georgie takes a job with the CBC

energy again and was alive with dreams of a special edition about the north country that they could produce from Lillooet. Margaret, however, had a more elaborate plan. She proposed changing the name of the *Howe Sound News* to the *Alaska Highway News* and publishing it in Fort St. John.

George reminded her of a little thing called the Wartime Prices and Trade Board that provided a set quota of newsprint. Ethically, he added, it was a stretch.

They had a quota to produce a paper for Squamish not Fort St. John. Just changing the name of the masthead seemed like cheating. Margaret quickly replied, "Well, we're not asking for anything more than the paper quota we already have. *Howe Sound News* is through. The north end of the province is just starting and they need a paper. Morally, it's right. And you know it's right. Leave it to God. Argue later." Margaret was always leaving her life in the hands of the unseen, calling on saints to protect bald tires, find lost keys, or (as in Shanghai) produce a little extra money in a pinch.

The call of the north won out and George went along with Margaret's plan. He immediately returned to the Peace River country to begin selling ads and subscriptions. Margaret produced the first issue of the *Alaska Highway News* out of Lillooet, printing it in Vancouver. When that was done she packed two old trunks with the bare necessities. Most of it was what one would need to produce a paper in the bush: envelopes, letterhead, mailing lists, and copy paper. She threw in some pillows, a feather tick, and a frying pan for good measure and made her way to Edmonton where George was waiting.

On the way up to Fort St. John, they found themselves fighting upstream (like salmon in a run) as thousands of American soldiers flowed out of the north bound for more exotic theatres of war. The preparation work for the highway had been completed and the military were heading back. Civilians were left to do the rest of the work, to surface the highway, to build the bridges, to lay the pipeline.

The sudden arrival and subsequent rapid departure of the U.S. military left Fort St. John in chaos. The sleepy hamlet of a hundred or so had exploded over a short 10 days into a community of 10,000. The gargantuan efforts of the U.S. Army to punch the road in eight months and 12 days brought a miraculous transformation of the virginal northern landscape that pushed bulldozers as far as the remote post of Fort Nelson before spring break-up. The economic transformation of Fort St. John was just as miraculous. This community — desperate with the poverty of the Depression — switched to prosperity within a single army pay period. The tumult of enterprise was staggering.

The district's citizens had adapted in a heartbeat. They moved from their houses and rented them out while they themselves moved into tents. They turned living rooms into cafés and bedrooms into bordellos. Farmhouses suddenly became parka factories or ice cream plants. Hospital staff chucked ward work to run a laundry. Secretaries became waitresses because the pay was better. If there was something to sell or a service demanded, the town citizens did their best to comply. The farming folk crammed their granaries in preparation for a road on which they could move their product to southern markets. Everyone quickly learned how to shake the American money tree to catch the fruit of the windfall. Rights to cross land went for $15 a half-hectare. Special military requests for extra beer usually required a little consideration in return. Kegs of nails. Stacks of lumber. The supply of cool drinks for the bull-dozer operators was paid for with boards for sidewalks in town, and the labour to build them.

George was able to secure a cottage-roofed frame house as an office for the new newspaper that would also serve as their home. This feat was just short of a miracle, considering the demand for space in Fort St. John. A Public Roads Administration employee had to pay $60 a month for a chicken house so he had a place for his wife to sleep — and the Husky Café had a snap-shot of the "only empty premises in town" — a bird-house.

The Murray's first Fort St. John home had been occupied by a Department of Transport engineer. It was a quickly-knocked-together oblong structure with little but a roof to recommend it. Nonetheless, it was suitable for the Murrays. A bed and a stove were borrowed and, with a 200-litre drum for water at the back door and orange crates from the butcher, the living quarters and news office were complete. Margaret set up a folding army table in the living-room to serve as a desk. She turned a chocolate box into a cash register, and used two saw-horses with planks for a counter. It didn't ever take much to put her in business. Her sensible adaptations weren't unique in Fort St. John. The whole area was raw, western, and makeshift. There were no lawns (except at the hospital) and no trees for shade. It was the perfect backdrop for the down-home style newspaper they were so adept at producing.

But, despite all their efforts, the Murrays had a struggle ahead of them to convince the people they needed Margaret's weekly dose of news. And getting the harried business people to part with some cash for advertising took all of her ingenuity.

Next door to the newspaper office, Ed Cuthill ran a busy meat market, which supplied beef, pork, and chicken to households across the northwest. When Margaret appeared at his counter ready to pitch white space, she found him up to his elbows in sausage meat. "Why sure," he answered when she asked for an ad. "You can put me down for a two-by-three advert. I'd make it more but I can't get help and I'm doing all the business I can handle." Margaret noticed crates of chickens in the back, waiting to be dispatched and plucked. "You make this ad a two-by-five and I'll come over and dress those chickens myself," she offered. Later, with pots of boiling water at the ready, Margaret axed, plucked, and gutted 29 birds, with George helping out on seven more. If that was what it would take to get the paper rolling, then Margaret was ready and willing.

George also reached back to earlier days in order to squeeze out advertising support but his talents were less agrarian. The town barber had been forced into a ticket system to handle his ever-present line of customers so George took up comb and scissors. He used every tea towel, sheet, and apron Margaret had stuffed in the trunks. As a spinoff George developed a fast track to the community gossip and news.

Chapter 6
The Dust Settles on Politics

F or the first two years of its life, the *Alaska Highway News* owed much of its existence to the Canadian Pacific Airline (CPA) pilots who flew to Fort St. John. Every Sunday they carried the bundle of news copy to Vancouver and every Wednesday their planes returned with the folded papers. It wasn't a perfect system. Sometimes the newspapers would find themselves in St. John's, Newfoundland. Or St. John, New Brunswick. Or Fort St. James. Other times, like luggage, they went missing forever. But, the system worked most of the time.

Much like the beginnings in Lillooet, the convoluted

process of publishing resulted in a high percentage of errors. When George was in Fort St. John and Margaret in Vancouver, the copy was formal and its grammar precise. With Margaret at the helm in the north and George in the south, readers were treated to quite the opposite. Margaret always managed to inject her own "voice" in the stories she wrote. District news that would have come out dry and factual from George's hand transformed to copy that literally dripped its distinct character off the pages and into readers' laps. She described a trip to Edmonton this way. "What do passengers do while a CPA Lodestar wings its way through the blue? They shoot craps. Altitude 6000 feet, temperature 55-below, bright sun, speed 200 miles an hour. The stewardess passed Spearmint gum. The 'Highwaymen' all have a carton of their favourite brand. Puff, chew, talk, laugh, seven-come-eleven. 'Be good to me, Baby....' I got out at Grande Prairie and a cadaverous Chinese took my seat. He had made a fortune at Dawson Creek and was on his way to do some shopping in Edmonton. Game resumed in the rotunda of the airport during the stop. Gentlemanly Canadian Air Force boys tiptoed gingerly across windows of folding money as the ivories galloped."

With all the antics that went on in Fort St. John and the surrounding district, the newspaper practically wrote itself in its first year. The Murrays invited local contributions and they got them. Everything from reports of bears to the size of the turnips being harvested. The form the paper took was created consciously by George and Margaret. They believed a good weekly newspaper should mirror its community, warts and all.

There was no formal announcement made when the American army began its complete withdrawal from Fort St. John in 1944. The Letters to the Editor column however, told the story as soldiers wrote in to buy subscriptions or say farewell. Margaret's newspaper was all kisses and hugs for the Yankee boys until the army faced the problem of equipment. They had moved a tremendous amount of material north for the highway construction, and on leaving had to figure out a way to remove it. Their decision was to dump, burn, and smash. Margaret was appalled.

In equipping the army, manufacturers in the United States scandalously over-supplied everything. It has been estimated that 14,000 pieces of heavy equipment, then valued at more than $10 million, disappeared from the highway project from 1942 to 1945. It simply went missing and no one was ever held accountable.

What was not important enough to be shipped back to the United States was stockpiled in depots along the highway for demolition. The army went into a frenzy of destruction with sledgehammers and wrecking bars. They burned, they crushed, and they buried. Everything from washing machines to bedding was pushed into coulees and covered by bulldozers. What was stockpiled became a tempting target for the 1000 or so thrifty permanent residents of the Peace River district, but the RCMP and the FBI made short work of anyone who was caught pilfering.

Margaret used the pages of her paper to warn readers against breaking the law, then pointed them to spots where the pickings were easy. She wasn't encouraging theft. Rather, she was promoting the conservation of these supplies for the people who would remain once the army departed. She even got in to the act herself. On one occasion, with her priest Father Youngbluth, and his fishing rod, she visited the town dump to witness the destruction of more goods than she'd ever seen in one place. Margaret, offering encouragement, helped the good priest guide a makeshift hook and line fashioned with haywire from a ridge overlooking the dump. They caught a pair of rubber boots, then a bale of mackinaws, and another and another, all destined for the Moberly Lake Natives.

Only the need to maintain silence and wartime security stopped her from protesting loudly about the shameless wastefulness that the U.S. Army was demonstrating. It kept her awake at night. It stung her frugal Irish upbringing.

If she wasn't able to publish the truth in Fort St. John, she reasoned, perhaps the papers in Vancouver might be interested. The *Vancouver Province* dispatched a reporter but the coverage made no difference to the army orders. The goods were all duty-free and therefore had to be destroyed. It was a travesty of waste Margaret was never able to forget.

The army's departure might have signaled a swift end to the prosperity had it not been for the civilians with families and the Canadian military who streamed in to fill the void. After them the oil scouts arrived. For over 20 years mineral surveys had identified the possibility of oil and gas under the muskeg. Now the road made these riches accessible. Until the government reserve on the land was lifted in 1947, the oil scouts had little to report, officially, but the Murrays told the stories of strikes anyway. In Pouce Coupe, a water driller hit a pocket of wet gas and that was all it took for George and Margaret to reprise every such accidental find recorded in the region since the 1920s. They did the stories, not because they wanted to lure the oil industry north, but because the finds proved them right. The north would not be returning to an economy of trappers. Its future was going to be just as George had predicted.

During the years that followed, George continued to lambaste the provincial government for its neglect. "The dead and distant hand of officialdom very often throttles local activity and blacks out the flame of progress. Northern British Columbia has closer ties with Edmonton than with Victoria," he wrote. Margaret went one better. She published a vote coupon in the paper and asked readers to mark their ballots for secession to Alberta. More than a quarter of her readers replied with a yes. Victoria however, still didn't take any serious notice.

George decided to take his fight for district recognition to the lion's den itself. The coalition between the Liberals and Conservatives created during the war years was no longer necessary in 1945, he editorialized. The two parties spent all their time being friendly to each other rather than concern themselves with the plight of the electorate. The government had more money in the bank than it did when the province joined Confederation. Its surplus stood at $45 million, yet nothing was being applied to roads or service improvements in the north.

Rumours were circulating that the government wanted to make the coalition permanent by creating a single new, merged party. And that threw Margaret into a fit.

"Over my dead body," she said. "I'll fight them with every breath I've got."

A provincial election was due in October, and that August the Liberals hurriedly called a convention to settle the issue of coalition. Both the Murrays attended the rather sedate confab at the Hotel Vancouver and tried to rouse a small band of party stalwarts to put the kybosh on the coalition plan. Premier Hart, however, had a stronger following. He spoke to the resolution and asked the convention to endorse it. When no one in their rebel group would stand to argue, Margaret did. "John Hart!" she shouted from the floor. "Mr. Hart, you are doing something today that will end the Liberal Party in British Columbia. If you decide on this treacherous course, it will not return in my lifetime, nor in yours."

George could see in Margaret's face that she was only getting started. She was going to make a spectacle of herself in his estimation and he held up a hand to silence her. Margaret saw the hand and visibly turned crimson. "George Murray, you'll not shush me this time. I will have my say." Her voice broke and she began to cry. "Who am I? A foot-slogger is what I am. A blotter-carrier — a canvasser — and for a party that hardly existed before 1912 in this province."

A woman offered up a derisive comment. Margaret

Ma Murray

Ma Murray with sledgehammer in hand at
the opening of the Fort St. John railroad terminal

turned towards the voice and abruptly told the woman to be quiet. "In 1916, I wasn't canvassing for the same thing you were," she said. The crowd may have thought the put-down a classic, but Margaret's pleas to the group to maintain their status went unheeded anyway. And the Murrays declared their own war.

George hustled back to his old riding in Lillooet and placed his name on the ballot as a Liberal Independent. Premier Hart quickly tried to deflate George's campaign with a notice in the *Vancouver Sun*. "George M. Murray has offered himself as a candidate for the Liberal Party in the riding of Lillooet. This is to advise the electors of this province that there is no Liberal Party in British Columbia."

Margaret returned to the north, but instead of mimicking George, turned to the Social Credit Party for a nomination. She admitted she didn't understand the tenets of that party, only that it offered an alternative to "that lame-brained outfit we have in Victoria."

George was utterly shattered by the news of his wife's defection. In a letter that October he told her how he felt. "I feel very much like the man who invented the atomic bomb. It was a great idea at the time, but now what to do with it? It may destroy all of us. Your announcement, of course, has eclipsed me in this campaign. If I spent money like water and spread publicity all over this place, I don't think it would do me any good at all."

Margaret replied with a volley of her own. "You force me to make my own decisions. You seem very lukewarm on this political setup. You are not ready to toss in the sponge and neither am I. I implore you to shake yourself into action. In two weeks it will be too late. Things are in a hell of a mess in the province. Don't you think you owe it to B.C. to do what you can?"

Dan, who had returned from the war to Lillooet, had dived right in to revitalizing the *Bridge River–Lillooet News*. He took what his mother had done personally. Dan promptly reserved space on the front page to denounce his mother and told the world she had nothing to do with the *News*. In fact, he said she was related to the family only by blood.

The Murrays took their politics very seriously, but no one in the north actually took Margaret that way. Though they lined up to hear her speak, she was more an entertainment than a possible representative solution. She had them laughing in the aisles and pouring over her editorials. But they had no intention of voting for her.

When the dust settled on the election, neither Murray had gained a seat. Both were forced back into using their newspapers to call for change and government largess around Lillooet and Fort St. John.

Chapter 7
An Attempted Retirement

After the election catastrophe, the Murrays were beginning to feel their age. Both were peeking at 60 and, with their two children now back in Canada, they decided it was time to split the empire and retire. Dan became the publisher in Lillooet. Georgie took the helm in Fort St. John. It was fine, in concept.

While George let Dan run his business without much interference, Georgie still had to contend with the ever-present shadow of Margaret. Her mother continued to write copy with its dangling participles, misspelled words, and sometimes confusing logic.

Ma Murray enjoying a joke

Margaret tried to leave the paper three times and three times "Ye Ed" returned.

The family had used Georgie's government-backed loans to establish a new plant and press, but turning over the reins of the business seemed an impossibility for Margaret. "We have a thousand subscribers now and it won't be long before we can pay her off," she'd loudly whisper to George, usually well within her daughter's hearing. "And besides, how can we retire? We haven't the money to retire. And who wants to, anyway?"

Georgie would just sigh and carry on, maintaining a quiet demeanor about it all. Though tempers sometimes erupted into loud arguments, the business of the paper continued to hum regardless of the ownership squabbles and Margaret's ever more distant retirement. In the post war years, the *Alaska Highway News* blossomed under Georgie's guidance, but it owed much of its popularity to her mother's constant sensational contributions.

It was about this time that Margaret decided to add a sticker to the overdue subscription notices on both newspapers, a trademark in a sense. "A chuckle once a week and a belly laugh once a month" was promised if the readers paid their bills.

It seemed that only Margaret ever really knew the current finances at the paper. She hung on to her account scribblers as fervently as she did her notebook. The money she had sole access to was doled out without asking anyone's approval. It went for small real estate speculations, for needy subscribers, and for her many other causes. She did it all, never considering it necessary to pay her daughter, the publisher, a fair wage. The printing staff was paid. The postman was paid. Even the boy who scraped ice from the stoop was paid. But Georgie was expected to work at the paper for the joy of it all and a roof over her head. After all, she was family.

As Fort St. John grew, Margaret took up the gauntlet for municipal services. The community needed water, she claimed. No water, no incorporation. From the time they'd arrived in Fort St. John, and accepted its delivery to a barrel at the back door, water had been a problem in the Murray household. It was still being delivered by wagon prior to Christmas 1947 when the village was finally incorporated, but at least a formal municipal supply was assured from then on.

That Christmas, Dan came to Fort St. John to discuss something important. He owned half of the interest in the *Bridge River-Lillooet News* just as Georgie supposedly owned half of the *Alaska Highway News*. He'd decided he wanted to sell out and move to California.

Margaret, who'd been sitting with one leg elevated on a footrest in the living-room when she heard, was in too much pain to stand. A motor mishap that resulted in battery acid being spilled over her ankles had left deep weeping ulcers that never healed properly for the rest of her life. So standing was difficult — but she could shout well enough.

"California? Infamy! Infamy!" She pounded the floor with her good foot. "That indolent, artificial, stultifying California! Where old people go to die! Where the flowers do not smell — only the movie stars! Where you live in a little house on a street with a hundred other little houses on a hundred other little streets and carry your lunch in a briefcase...." She was so furious she had to search for the words to continue. "And all this God-given opportunity right at your feet, this glorious north, this wonderful Peace River country, these splendid people...."

Dan only smiled. He wanted to make more money and his wife Kathleen wanted to go. She was a cultured city girl and Lillooet had never been her cup of tea. To Dan, a newspaper should exist for the publisher's purse first and the advertiser second. Readers were only an incidental requirement in the formula.

In the early years of the war, George had converted the log cabin on the *Bridge River–Lillooet News* property (the one that had been used as a stable for camels during the Cariboo gold rush) into a theatre. Dan had to sweep the aisles of popcorn one too many times for his liking, when he should have been publishing the paper. In his preparations to divest himself of the newspaper, Dan sold the Log Cabin Theatre to the Canadian Legion and turned the proceeds over to his parents. Then he burned everything he didn't want from the newspaper office, and was ready to sell the paper.

Margaret couldn't fathom what was going through Dan's mind. He had an inheritance in the paper for heaven sake. She connived a little to try and entice him to accept her legacy by cajoling Georgie to quit. What she said to her daughter was tried and true Margaret Lally blather. "This newspaper holds no future for you, Georgie," she said. "The only proper career for a woman, after all, is marriage. Just fill my arms with grandchildren is all I ask." How could her mother stand before the young woman and claim a newspaper was no place for a woman? It was ludicrous, facile, and insulting. To anyone but Georgie, her mother's obvious scheme might have been the catalyst for family separation.

Luckily a twist of fate saved the two Murray women from a terribly sad parting. It arrived in the form of Sergeant Major James Keddell. The sergeant major appeared at the news office to deliver a bottle of overproof rum for the editor and Margaret immediately turned into a matchmaker. Just 10 weeks from the day that the boy from Three Hills, Alberta tromped into the news office and made his delivery, Georgie became his wife.

It took almost a year for Dan to complete the newspaper sale in Lillooet. Georgie had left Fort St. John immediately after the wedding, bound for the army's married quarters in Whitehorse. This didn't work to change Dan's mind though. What did throw a crimp into the California plan however, was his father's decision to run for office as the member of parliament in Peace River.

George was running as a Liberal but having the shadow of a turncoat Socred on the family reputation was going to make a win more difficult. To help the cause, Margaret agreed to "disappear for a while." She volunteered to travel to Whitehorse and boost for Aubrey Simmons, the Liberal candidate there. So, while George campaigned in British Columbia and his mother helped Simmons garner votes in the gulches of the Yukon — Dan took over the *Alaska Highway News.*

Margaret had explained her reasons to Dan with typical bluntness. "Up here they don't know I'm tainted," she said. "Besides, Aubrey can't speak for sour apples and he needs me." And that was that. Two weeks of campaigning in a little single-engine aircraft lay ahead.

Because the plane was a piston-banger on its last legs, Margaret was forced to travel light but evidently not light enough. Her baggage usually consisted of candidate Simmons and a travelling case. On one flight, gaining altitude came down to dumping either the campaign literature or Margaret's luggage. Margaret obliged, stuffing her "unmentionables" into a paper bag and heaving the rest. On another, she had to rip away part of her slip to make a stopper for a leaking pontoon.

At 62 years of age, clothes weren't a big concern for Margaret. She tromped about in a $150 black coat and her support hose, from dining halls to creek beds. She used every electioneering trick she'd learned. She talked to workers who simply couldn't escape if they wanted to — she bought rounds in beer parlors — then bribed owners to lock the doors while she spoke. She was something hard to describe.

Margaret Fielder, a CBC reporter who was with her in Dawson City made an attempt. "She made an eerie picture in that trailing chiffon nightie on the slanting boards of the first floor of the Royal Alexandra Hotel in Dawson. The ornate hallway to the bathroom heaved like the deck of a ship. No rooms with bath of course. And then her sitting in this outfit, glass in hand, recounting the day's experiences on the campaign trail."

While Simmons' campaign was one for the history books, George's version in the Cariboo riding was staid and reserved. He won it anyway and in June 1949 became an MP.

During George's term of office in Ottawa, Margaret stayed close to the *News.* In spite of her pledges that Dan could assume his heritage, she still refused to let go. Dan worked hard, seven days a week. He cleaned up the circulation, put a clerical eye to the accounting, and demanded professionalism from all the staff. Even so, Margaret signed nothing over. She held the pledge of ownership like a carrot. Dan finally gave up and left.

In the months that followed, George reported on Ottawa and his progress in gaining funding for telephones or roads. Margaret replied with details about her time putting out the paper alone. "We had $400 biz this week and it cost $330 to produce. This latest printer you sent is the biggest blank of all the blanks I have met yet and that's a few. He eats bread, butter, and honey with his potatoes and meat. You might as well feed a calf. He is what we used to call a blue belly Yank. He might have done a fine job of brushing you off in the men's room. The point is, how do I do a fine job of brushing him off here? You should never drink anything stronger than coffee."

Back and forth, letter after letter, it was much the same for Margaret. She missed the dear man in her life and saw in his correspondence how being a backbencher troubled him. George couldn't wield influence and without it little could happen. He was a man who wanted to see his dreams for the north country fulfilled, but he just couldn't move the moribund Parliament his way more than a few inches. At home in Fort St. John, Margaret read his speeches in Hansard and wept.

But, while George may not have been setting the world on fire with his fight for the Peace River country or Asia–Pacific trade, he was still considering running again. He had made enough progress for his electorate to justify their faith for a second time.

It was then that Margaret, through some fault of her own, made a mark that rocked the family from California to Ottawa. She talked to Earl Beattie and he wrote an article about her for *Chatelaine Magazine*. Overnight the legend of "Ma" Murray was born.

The article Beattie penned was colourful, well written, and more-or-less factual, but it described Margaret as a female frontier caricature of the woman she really was. It hinted she was courageous but left the intimation she was foolhardy. It described her like a cardboard cutout of other "Ma" legends in the Canadian northwest. Suddenly Margaret became the kind of woman who could chew gunpowder and wash it down with whiskey.

George, who was always sensitive to the opinions of others and especially so where it concerned Margaret, was devastated. Now, not only did he have to fight the skeleton of a Socred in his bed, the legend had a nickname.

Chapter 8
A Final Parting

hen the Liberals and Conservatives decided to form a coalition government in British Columbia it was to prevent what they feared would be a socialist Co-operative Commonwealth Federation sweep. On the coalition's failure, six years after Margaret had tearfully pleaded against its formation, she practically shouted her "I told you so" in the newspaper. "The shotgun marriage using CCF ammunition has broken up. The coalition government has come apart. It lasted six years and knocked colder'n a mackerel both Liberals and Conservatives except federally. There isn't a grassroots organization for

either one of them left. Membership has been stifled. And now we must pick up the pieces. The miracle is that it didn't get to be a den of thieves long ago. But it didn't. And we have had good government, withal."

She was right about the electorate. Instead of turning back to the old parties, voters put a hardware store operator from Kelowna named W.A.C. Bennett, and his Social Credit Party, in shaky power. Margaret, of course, gave the new government with its young politicians barely a week without one criticism or another. The popularity she had suddenly found with the identifiable nickname of "Ma" required her to push the envelope as it were. Her speeches became a little saltier, her editorials a little more folksy.

In the spring of 1951, she and George attended a Joint International Committee of Chambers of Commerce of the United States and Canada with 100 other delegates. As the delegate who had travelled the furthest for the gathering, Margaret was invited to say a few words — three minutes worth — at the end of the meeting. She took to the lectern and after introducing herself as having come from a point closer to Siberia than Irvington, West Virginia (where the meeting was being held) promptly warned the distinguished audience that they had better help develop the north before China decided to invade.

"Do you realize that unless you help us to do something about developing our country, the Orientals will come across that tiny Bering Sea and take this northern land of ours?" Of course, the crowd was taking her words with a liberal amount of salt, but when the chairman said her time was up the audience didn't agree. To their urging she continued. She told them how she'd moved to Canada from Kansas and married George. "George Murray was working for northern development then, in 1912. He is still working for it. And as you ladies here know — when a good woman gets under a man — he moves!"

The crowd erupted with howling laughter which encouraged Ma Murray, "We grow everything big in the Peace," she said, pushing out her chest. With that move the top button on her dress popped. Now the crowd was literally falling from their chairs. When George was asked to conclude the meeting, they both received a standing ovation.

By the late fall of 1952, both Georgie and Dan were back at the paper, helping their mother who had turned 64 that August. Another election was looming and Margaret was helping George, though his prospects were poor. The electorate was fat, happy, and preoccupied. He lost by 400 votes.

Life around the Murray household and the paper

was gloomy. Dan once again tried to run the newspaper efficiently and at a profit. Margaret continued to rile him at every turn. Nothing had changed. Margaret was still right and the world was still wrong, he said. And again, Dan packed up and left. This time he wouldn't return without terms — in writing. Margaret just couldn't understand her son's desire to make money. To her it was a mystery. "Cut off my hand at the wrist if I know who in the world he takes after," she said to her ever-attentive daughter who knew his departure would mean an extra load of work.

Eventually the desire to see her son inherit and carry on their newspaper dream took precedence. Negotiations were conducted by mail. They sold Dan controlling interest in the *Alaska Highway News* on Georgie's suggestion. She settled for 25 percent of the legacy she'd once been promised.

Dan instituted financial control — and while the paper was much more like the profitable ones he wanted to emulate — it lost its fire. Without Margaret's lurid copy and George's eloquent editorials, it no longer carried the special voice of the northern wilderness the couple loved. The newspapering couple watched its transformation reluctantly, in silence. Until Dan, for the sake of economy, decided to pull the Fort Nelson page from the editorial line-up. It would not return, Dan told his furious mother, until it could pay for itself.

For Margaret, it was a stab into the heart of everything she'd struggled to build. She and George had never published for the sake of money alone. They'd worked hard, almost every day, for one simple reason. They had worked for the thrill of exposing the jewels of joy hidden in the lives of their readers.

With a few well-phrased curses, Margaret caught the bus to Fort Nelson. Though she was 71 and in constant pain from her ulcerated ankle, she hit the sidewalks one more time to gather news and sell ads. She managed to produce five thin four-page issues of the *Fort Nelson News*, without anyone else's help. With each issue, a special complimentary copy she personally addressed as "free" was mailed to Dan. But the years had caught up with her and before she could publish her sixth edition, she collapsed.

In the summer that followed, George cared for Margaret and they returned to Lillooet with a new dream. The Murrays bought back the old Lillooet newspaper premises, the linotype and press, the type cases, and the tables. But this time their plan did not involve publishing. Perhaps with some work, they could turn the old building into a trade school. Perhaps with some luck, there would be young people eager enough to come to Lillooet to learn about what it takes to publish a weekly. Neither George nor Margaret was truly certain they still had the energy, but at the same time neither was willing to admit that age had stolen their will to try.

Later that week, on his way back to Fort St. John to complete their move, George missed a curve and his car plunged down a 35-metre bank. George survived the accident, but he was taken to the hospital in Vancouver for treatment. There it was discovered he'd been hiding a malignancy from the family for years and he died from its affects on August 19, 1961. They buried him in Fort St. John. Margaret didn't shed a tear.

Dan delayed that week's edition so his mother could write George's obituary herself. "He was our light and life and inspiration. We will never have the depth or the girth of his lovely heart and fine mind, and our flap-doodle vernacular or daring courage only came from the inward security he gave us."

Then she left for Lillooet and from there on a trip to Ontario to see George's family. Her trip turned into a whirlwind of luncheon engagements and interviews that lasted until the end of October. Through it all she still hadn't grieved for George.

When she finally got back to Lillooet, she purpose-fully climbed the stairs to the living quarters and flung open the upper door. There, on the hall tree, was

George's coat and hat. There, in the dark silence of that old building, Margaret finally managed to cry.

Epilogue

Margaret could never pull herself from the thrill of a deadline for long. With faithful daughter Georgie always near, she managed to breathe new life into the dead *Bridge River-Lillooet News* after George passed away. Her editorials were a caustic mix of humour and wisdom, full of bad spelling and poor grammar. To Margaret, syntax was something you paid to the church. Instead of worrying, she simply added a block of shuffled letters and invited readers to add the ones she'd missed.

Ma Murray received the Order of Canada in 1971 and was awarded an honorary doctorate from Simon Fraser University that same year. The accolades didn't change her one iota.

She continued to write about the comings and goings in the village and her "Chat Out of the Old Bag" column until she was 85. Finally, failing health forced her to sell the paper. Her tenacious will and outspoken journalism still continues to inspire the community newspaper industry three decades later.

Her plain speaking was quoted in *Time* Magazine

and *Maclean's*. She was hosted on CBC's *Front Page Challenge* twice. Her own half-hour, twice a month television program followed. Her life, with all its highs and lows, inspired a hit play by Eric Nichol that drew packed houses nationwide. Parts of her editorials criticizing greedy politicians or unfair laws were reprinted by newspapers across the country. Premier W.A.C. Bennett visibly cringed at the mention of her name. She was either loved or reviled. There were never lukewarm opinions about the feisty old editor and she took in all the attention with a big smile and a "God bless you." Never rich in a material way, she was enormously wealthy where it counted most, in character.

Every night she climbed into her bed, just a shuffle down the hall from her tiny office, and pulled out a name from a tiny basket. It was always someone she knew needed "a little extra" from the God to whom she passionately prayed. Then, she might share a little of the news of her day with George. Perhaps sip some stout "to thicken the blood" — and try to sleep — her conscience clear.

Margaret Lally "Ma" Murray passed away in that bed above the old Lillooet news office on September 25, 1982. She was 94. With all the angels that watched over her, it's certain she didn't die alone.

A play celebrating the life of the feisty Ma Murray
premiered in Kamloops in 1981.

Bibliography

Beattie, Earle. "The Rebel Queen of the Northwest" in *Chatelaine.* Vol. 25, no. 5, May 1952.

Bridge River–Lillooet News. *'Ma' Murray's Birthday Scrapbook.* Lillooet, July 31, 1996.

Green, Lewis. *The Great Years.* Vancouver: Tricouni Press, 2000.

House, Jackson. "Ma Murray: The Salty Scourge of Lillooet." in *Maclean's.* Vol. 79, March 19, 1966.

Keddell, Georgina. *The Newspapering Murrays.* Toronto: McClelland & Stewart Ltd., 1967.

British Columbia Weekly Newspapers Association. "Ma Murray's Bridge River-Lillooet News" in *A History of Weekly Newspapers of British Columbia.* Mission: British Columbia Weekly Newspapers Association, 1972.

MacEwan, Grant. *Mighty Women: Stories of Western Canadian Pioneers.* Vancouver: Greystone Books, 1995.

Bibliography

O'Clery, Jean. "Murray, Margaret Teresa" in *The Canadian Encyclopedia*. Edmonton: Hurtig Publishers, 1988.

McCune, Shane. "The Mother of All Editors" in *Vancouver Province*, March 10, 1999.

Acknowledgments

The author would like to thank Georgina Keddell for writing her family history, *The Newspapering Murrays*. It's out-of-print but I encourage anyone interested in more detail on Margaret, George, Georgie, or Dan to find it. Georgie was a selfless saint, a mentor, and a special friend. Even after 30 years, I still miss her hearty laugh, her crazy stories, and her wisdom.

Thanks to Bain Gair of the *Bridge River—Lillooet News* for providing photographs and clippings. Thanks as well to fellow writer and Georgie's daughter, Margie Graham. I'm looking forward to someday reading her book on the chaotic life with the battling Murrays. Margie kindly permitted me the honour of retelling her grandma's story without influence or restriction and I'm grateful.

Finally, if she's listening…I want to thank my snuff-snorting friend, MLM, for the two years we shared as Lillooet scribes. I hope you, and the angel with "the heart of a bondswoman," approve.

About the Author

Stan Sauerwein lives and writes in Westbank, British Columbia. A freelance writer for two decades, his articles have appeared in a variety of Canadian and U.S. magazines and newspapers. Specializing in business subjects he has written for both corporations and governments. He is also the author of *Rattenbury: The Life and Tragic End of B.C.'s Greatest Architect* and *Fintry: Lives, Loves and Dreams.*

AMAZING STORIES™

ALBERTA TITANS

From Rags to Riches During
Alberta's Pioneer Days

HISTORY/BIOGRAPHY
by Susan Warrender

Alberta Titans
ISBN 1-55153-983-7

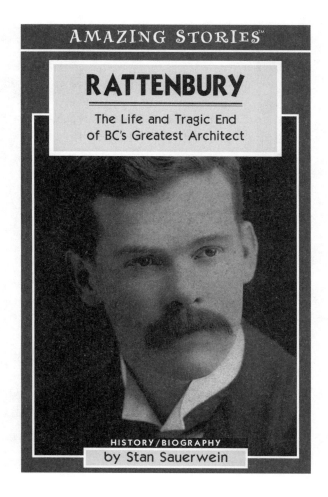

AMAZING STORIES™

RATTENBURY

The Life and Tragic End of BC's Greatest Architect

HISTORY/BIOGRAPHY
by Stan Sauerwein

Rattenbury
ISBN 1-55153-981-0

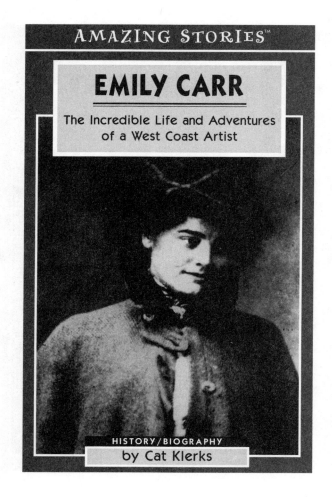
Emily Carr
ISBN 1-55153-996-9